GUITAR
DIAL 9-1-1

ISBN 0-634-00969-9

HAL•LEONARD®
CORPORATION
7777 W. BLUEMOUND RD. P.O. BOX 13819 MILWAUKEE, WI 53213

Visit Hal Leonard Online at **www.halleonard.com**

CONTENTS

HOW TO USE THIS BOOK

Just jump in anywhere! Each section is intended to stand by itself—as long as you know how to read tab, you're ready to go.

In general, the material in the beginning of the book is easier to play than the sections towards the end. However, regardless of the amount of technique a section requires, each contains some chords, licks, fingerings, or ideas that will be useful to players of all levels.

Although each section focuses on one skill, I will frequently refer to other figures and pages so that you can see how individual skills can be brought together. Often, many of the nearby sections will be related; for example, all the sections on blues progressions are near each other. So when you feel confident with a skill, just flip to a nearby page and you'll likely find some material that can be used with it.

Good Luck!

ACKNOWLEDGMENTS

I would like to give special thanks to my mother and father. I would also like to thank Howie Cohen, Kim Brooks, John Charles, John D'earth, Jim Kim, and Danny Siegel.

ABOUT THE AUTHOR

Ken has been teaching and performing for 15 years. He has published articles in *GuitarOne* magazine and has taught at the University of Virginia and the National Guitar Workshop. He has played with artists such as vocal legend Billy Eckstein and jazz guitarist Pat Metheny.

ABOUT THE RECORDING

The music on the CD is performed by Doug Boduch.

FINGERBOARD NOTE NAMES

In order to get the most out of the material that follows, you need to know the names of the notes at each fret on every string. Let's say a figure uses a G minor arpeggio (G–B♭–D) whose root is on the fourth string. You may like the sound of this arpeggio, but you want to know where it could be played as a Cm (C–E♭–G) arpeggio. So you need to know the names of the notes on this string in order to determine where the C is—and as the chart in Fig. 1 tells you, it's at the 10th fret.

One of the easiest ways to get this information is to keep the chart handy. It tells you the name of every note on the fingerboard. Memorizing this entire chart, though, might be tough. Often, knowing the names of the notes on the lowest two strings (E–A) is enough. Once you are familiar with these, you can easily figure out the names of the notes on the other strings by using a few simple octave shapes.

You can determine the name of any note on the fourth string by using an octave shape that refers you back to a note on the sixth string. If you want to figure out the name of the note on the fifth fret (the first note in Fig. 2), for example, you simply play that note with the third finger. Then, using the octave shape (from the diagram in Fig. 2), you play the corresponding note on the sixth string. Since you have memorized that note as a G (the last note in the figure), you know the note on the fifth fret is also a G.

Fig. 1

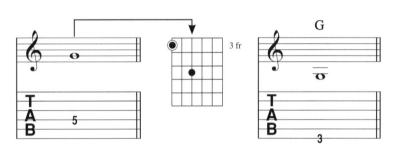

Fig. 2

To determine the names on the third string (such as the name of the note on the 6th fret in Fig. 3), you employ the same method and octave shape as in Fig. 2. This time, however, you start on a note on the third string and use the octave shape to refer back to the fifth string.

Fig. 3

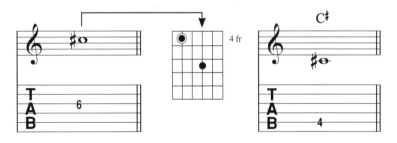

To determine notes on the second string (Fig. 4), you use a different octave shape, but the method will remain the same.

Fig. 4

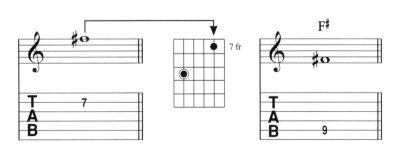

CHAPTER

ADDING THE 9TH

One of the quickest ways to give a chord a little color is to add the 9th—the tone found an octave plus a whole step above the chord's root. Fig. 5 uses this idea on the classic i–♭VII–♭VI progression (in E minor: Em–D–C). You can easily determine the 9th: its name is that of the note two frets above the root.

1 ▶ Fig. 5

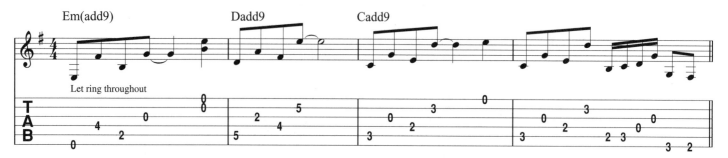

While conventional picking patterns often use consecutive strings, Fig. 5 features string skips. The beginning of measure 1, for example, moves from the sixth string to the fourth, then the fifth to the third. Because such patterns are less common, they will help to make your parts sound more original.

Though essentially the same progression as Fig. 5, Fig. 6 adds some variety by alternating between the add9 form and the basic chord. To create even more variety, I change the alternation: in measure 1, I start with the add9 and then switch to the Em; on the C, however, I reverse this pattern by beginning with the C and then moving to the add9.

2 ▶ Fig. 6

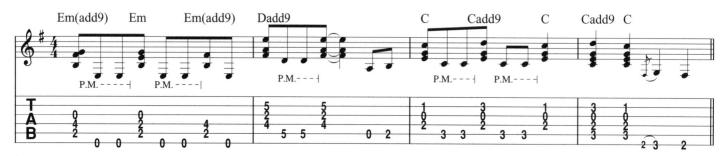

Fig. 7 employs a I–♭VI–♭VII–IV in A (A–F–G–D), but all of the add9 chords are played over the tonic note of the key (A).

3 ▶ Fig. 7

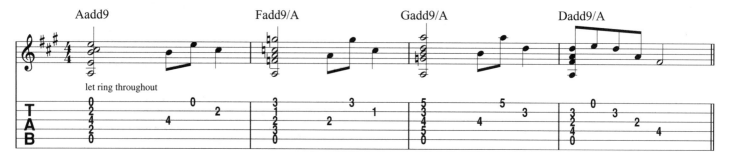

Fig. 8 gives you six movable add9 fingerings to experiment with. Some of these chords are a little difficult to play, but their unique texture makes it worth the effort.

Fig. 8

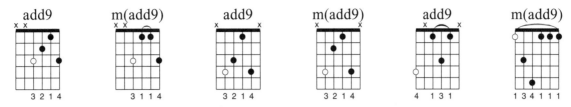

EXTRA POWERFUL POWER CHORDS

Players typically rely on power chords in the standard two- or three-note versions. But you can achieve an even more powerful sound for your riffs by using four-, five-, and six-note forms. Fig. 9 features seven power chords that each have at least four notes. Because many of these forms employ open strings, they can't be moved; the second A5, however, is a movable four-note form. The movable B♭5 and E♭5 differ from conventional power chords in that they have the fifth for the lowest note instead of the root; this produces an extremely thick-sounding chord. Check out measure 2 in Fig. 10.

Fig. 9

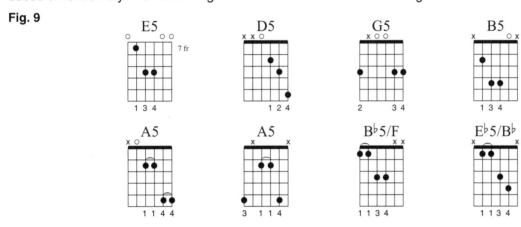

The first two measures of Fig. 10 apply some of the chords from Fig. 9 to one of the most frequently heard progressions I–♭VII–IV–I in E (E–D–A–E). In measures 3 and 4, you move from the I to the ♭III (G) and end by palm muting a series of notes from the E blues scale (E–G–A–B♭–B–D).

4 **Fig. 10**

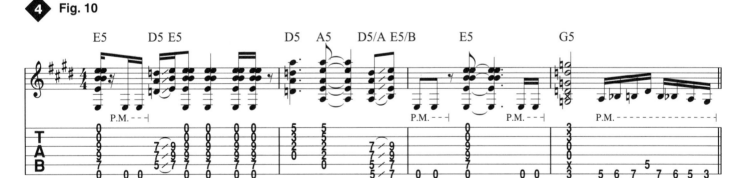

While power chords sound heaviest when the notes are played simultaneously, they also work well when arpeggiated. This is a method players and songwriters sometimes overlook. Fig. 11 arpeggiates power chords and adds connecting lines derived from the E natural minor scale (E–F♯–G–A–B–C–D).

5 **Fig. 11**

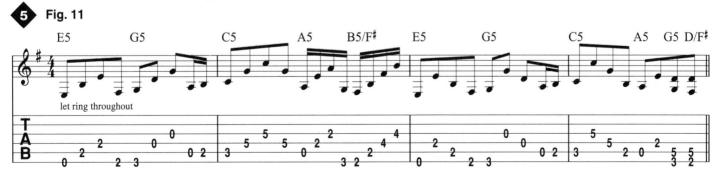

Based on the notes in the G blues scale (G–B♭–C–D♭–D–F), the dense riff in Fig. 12 combines power chords (played as chords and as arpeggios) with single-note lines. The first four fingerings in measure 1 are dyads—two notes played together. These dyads are two-note power chords, but the notes are inverted. In order, the dyads form F5, F♯5, G5, and B♭5 power chords.

6 Fig. 12

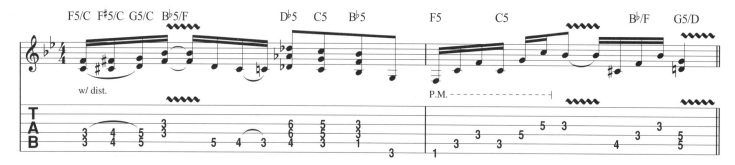

FAMILIAR CHORDS IN UNFAMILIAR PLACES

Chords that sound relatively tame in open position will often sound great when played at different frets. You can move any open position fingering up the fretboard; in Fig. 13 and Fig. 14, we'll use an open position G.

Based on the typical progression I–♭III–IV, Fig. 13 features the G played on the third, sixth, and eighth frets. When you move the chord to a new fret, the root is different, and because we are mixing in open strings (D and G), the chord type also changes: at the sixth fret, the chord becomes B♭6, and at the eighth fret, Cadd2.

7 Fig. 13

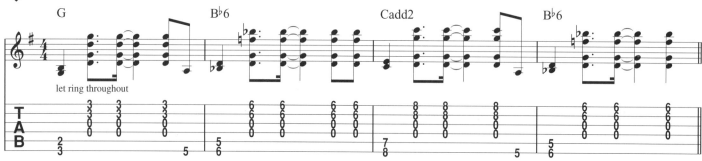

let ring throughout

Like any open position fingering, the G chord will not sound good at every fret. Here are two other places, though, where it works well: with the root at the fifth fret (A7add4) and at the tenth fret (Dadd4). Fig. 14 shows you these two chords plus two chords from Fig. 13. If we play the chords in Fig. 14 consecutively, they form a I–♭III–IV–♭VII progression. In the key of A, these chords are A, C, D, and G. When you work on this figure, make it a little more interesting by using the strumming patterns from Figs. 32A–33C (see *Strumming*), and the fingerpicking patterns from Chapter 2. Experiment with the order of the chords to create progressions in different keys. If you play Dadd4, Cadd2, G, A7add4, for example, you end up with a I–♭VII–IV–V in D.

Fig. 14

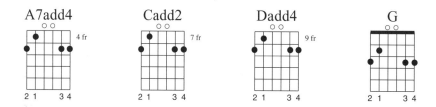

Fig. 15 is based on a different open position chord—an E (the voicing in measure 1). This chord sounds good at almost every fret, but in this figure we use it in five other locations. If you wanted, you could play any or all of the chords in this figure with the open 6th string (E) in the bass. To determine the name of each chord if you do this, simply replace the note after the slash (/) with E. When the Badd4/F♯ in measure 2 is played with the E in the bass, for example, it becomes Badd4/E. (Note: While the chord in measure 6 could be called G6/E, most players would likely refer to it as Em7.)

Fig. 15

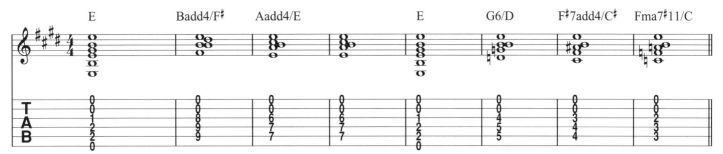

MORE FAMILIAR CHORDS IN UNFAMILIAR PLACES

Here, we apply the approach used in Figs. 13–15 to a number of other common chord fingerings.

The voicing in Fig. 16 comes from an F barre chord on the first fret. In this example, though, we use the voicing without the barre, playing the first two strings open.

 Fig. 16

The progression in Fig. 17 uses a familiar voicing—a three-note power chord. Here, we play the fingering at different frets and add the first two open strings (B and E) in order to create a number of very uncommon chord qualities. The chart in Fig. 18 tells you the name of this voicing at every fret. (The two frets marked with * above them are locations where the chord is rarely ever played.)

Fig. 17

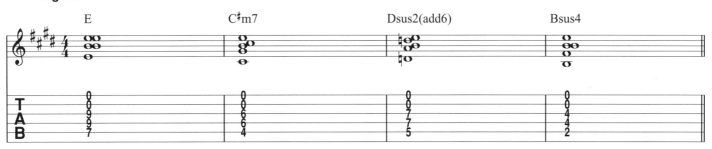

Fig. 18

	*				*						
1	2	3	4	5	6	7	8	9	10	11	12
B♭5(♭9)♯11	Bsus4	Cmaj7	C♯m7	Dsus2(add6)	E♭5♭9♯5	E5	Fmaj7♯11	F♯7sus4	G6	Emaj7/G♯	Asus2

Fig. 19 uses voicings from Fig. 18 along with some common chords.

Fig. 19

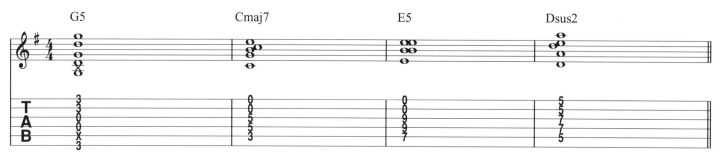

Fig. 20 includes four less-frequently played chord voicings that, like the chords in the previous examples, work well at many different frets. Again, experiment with each chord at every fret in order to determine which locations sound best.

Fig. 20

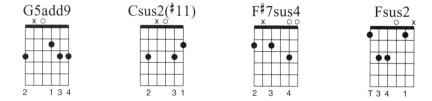

CLOSE VOICINGS WITH OPEN STRINGS

Sometimes it's difficult to play on the guitar the complex voicings we hear keyboard players use. But you can imitate these types of voicings by playing chords higher up the neck with open strings mixed in. Often, the results are chords that are voiced a lot closer than typical guitar chords. For instance, check out the Am(add9add4) in measure 1 of Fig. 22. It has four consecutive notes (B–C–D–E)—a voicing impossible to duplicate with any conventional open position or barre chord. Since guitarists use these kinds of chords less frequently, they will give your guitar parts an uncommon sound.

Fig. 21 is based on the progression I–IV–V–vi in E (E–A–B–C♯m). When you play the chord in the beginning of each measure, strum from the high string to the low, keeping the pick near the bridge for a brighter tone.

9 **Fig. 21**

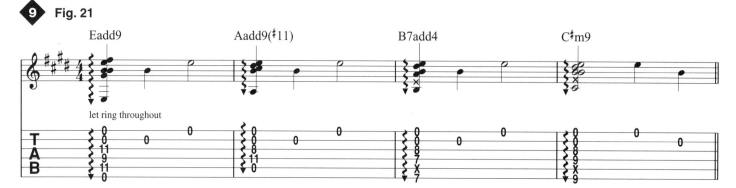

Fig. 22 employs a i–♭VI–iv–V progression. The picking pattern for this figure—all consecutive strings—is very conventional, yet because of the voicings it sounds as if you are often picking non-adjacent strings.

10 **Fig. 22**

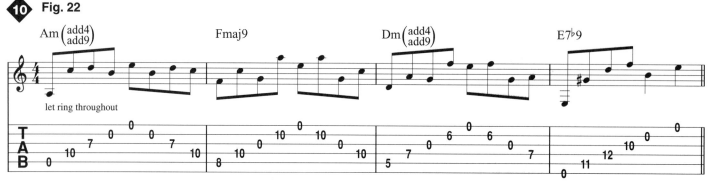

Another common set of changes, i–♭VII–♭VI–iv, serves as the basis for Fig. 23. When you play this figure, try some of the strumming patterns from Figs. 32A–33C (see *Strumming*).

Fig. 23

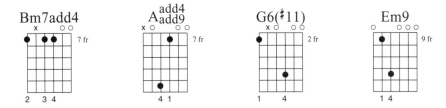

The voicings in Fig. 24 (I–♭VII–IV–♭VI–V in D) are unusual in that they have some large intervals between some of the inner notes in the chord. Like the close voicings in Figs. 21-23, these open voicings provide an alternative to typical guitar chords.

Fig. 24

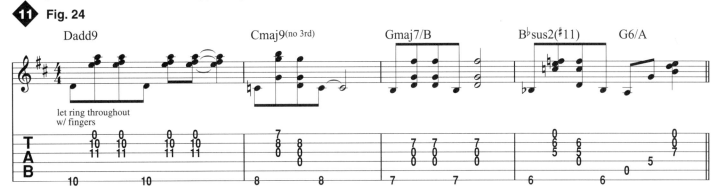

DIFFERENT VOICINGS OF THE SAME CHORD

When writing songs and making up guitar parts, we often fall into the "one voicing per chord" formula. If a song has a two-bar pattern—say, a measure of C to a measure of B♭—we tend to play only one fingering for each chord. Such a formula can be effective, but if relied on too often it can result in similar sounding parts. You can avoid this problem by creating riffs that move between different voicings of the same chord. The riff in Fig. 25, for example, uses multiple versions of the C and B♭ chords, as well as add9 and sus2 fingerings. Try it with a "down-down-up" strum pattern, as well as all downstrokes. Even something as simple as pick direction can have a big effect on the sound and feel of your riff.

Fig. 25

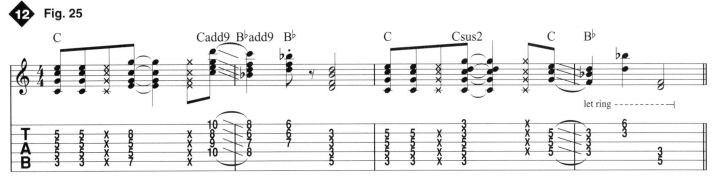

Fig. 26 is based on a I–IV progression in G (G–C). As in Fig. 25, this figure gives you some variety by using two versions of each chord. Try playing measure 1 two ways: using only downstrokes, then only upstrokes.

Fig. 26

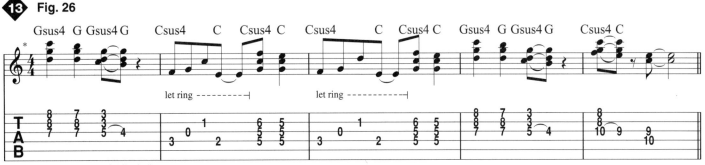

*Key Signature denotes G Mixolydian.

The use of inversions—chords with chord tones other than the root in the bass—will also diversify your parts. In Fig. 27, the overall harmony stays the same throughout each bar while the bass note shifts, adding some motion to the figure. These inversions allow you to play two chords in each measure by simply changing one note.

Fig. 27

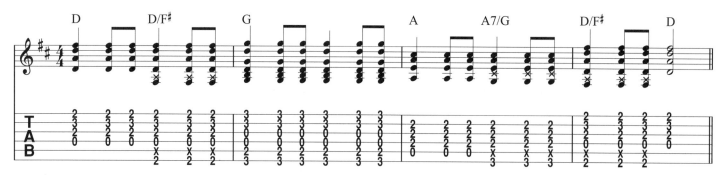

In Fig. 28A, you have three voicings of the same major triad. Fig. 28B gives you three voicings of the same minor triad. Figs. 28C and 28D use the same process on the next string grouping. Try using these different voicings to spice up your guitar parts. They'll provide some variety and motion that may have otherwise been lacking.

Fig. 28A – Major Triads

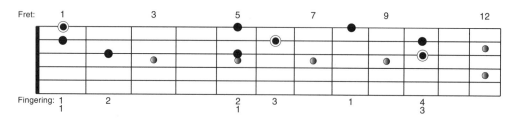

Fig. 28B – Minor Triads

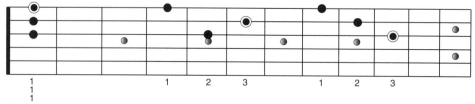

Fig. 28C – Major Triads

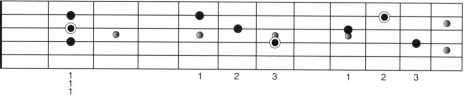

Fig. 28D – Minor Triads

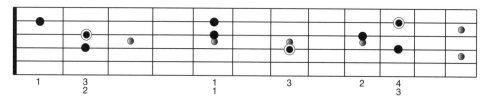

DRIVING BASS

Often, a progression which seems a little flat can be strengthened by playing each chord over the same bass note. Such a device is referred to as a *pedal tone*. This is easiest to do when using the open E (sixth), open A (fifth), or open D string (fourth) as your bass. Using a fretted bass note takes a little more effort. Fig. 29, for example, uses a low G as the pedal underneath a I–♭VI–♭VII–IV sequence in G (G–E♭–F–C). Notice how keeping the G in the bass requires a strange fingering for the F/G (unless you use your thumb for the low G).

Fig. 29

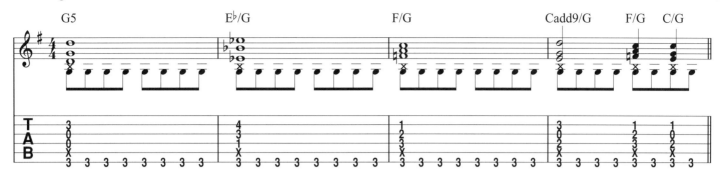

When guitarists use pedal tones, most often they choose the tonic note as the pedal: if the progression is in G, then they play the chords over a G note. But notes other than the tonic can work, too. The chords in Fig. 30 are very similar to those in Fig. 29, but they are played over a D, the fifth degree of the G scale.

Fig. 30

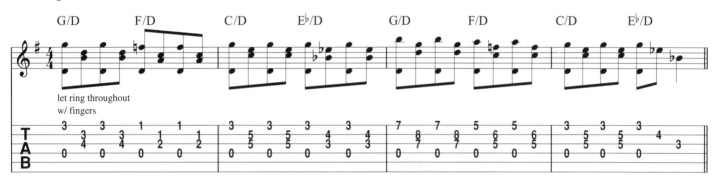

The A minor progression in Fig. 31 contains a different bass note in each measure. It also features a classic guitar move: a sus4 chord resolving to a major or minor triad.

 Fig. 31

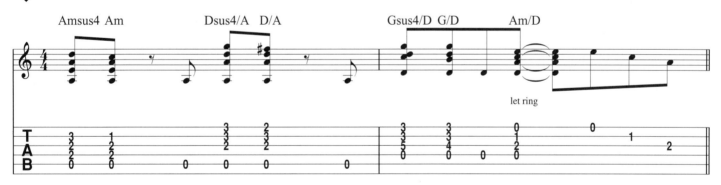

Try this technique with other progressions. As in Fig. 29, you might have to experiment with different fingerings to find the easiest way to play them. (You can get around any unconventional fingerings, however, by playing the chords with standard fingerings while a bassist plays the bass note.) Pedal tones can be helpful not only when creating guitar parts, but when thinking about your song as a whole. Songwriters often contrast the verse and the chorus by building one on a normal progression and the other on a pedal tone.

STRUMMING

Here we look at a few ways to make strumming patterns more interesting. This can be accomplished by changing pick direction and by muting strings with either the left or right hand. When you work on Figs. 32A–33C, apply the patterns to both open-position and barre chords.

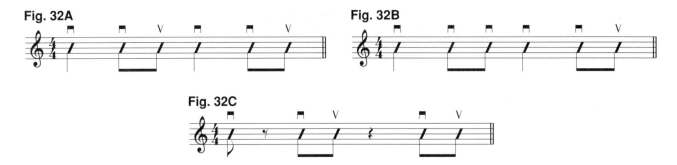

Fig. 32A   Fig. 32B

Fig. 32C

Figs. 33A and 33B share the same rhythmic pattern, but they use different picking patterns. Notice how this alters the sound. One reason for the change is that down picks tend to emphasize the lower notes in the chord and thus give the riff a heavier sound.

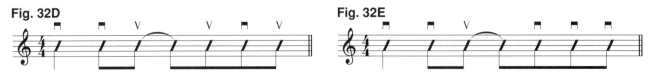

Fig. 32D   Fig. 32E

Fig. 33C uses a similar pattern, but here we add more space to the rhythm by stopping the chords from ringing. You can do this either by dampening the strings with the palm of the strumming hand or lightly lifting the fretting-hand fingers off the fingerboard and resting them on the strings. The latter method, however, will be more difficult when using open-position chords.

Fig. 32F

Figs. 33A–33C take the ideas in the above examples and apply them to another rhythmic pattern. Here, we will strum muted strings in order to get a percussive effect. The x's in the tablature in these figures indicate the muted strings that are played. You want to lightly lift your fingers off the fingerboard—they should be holding the chord shape, touching only the strings and not the fingerboard. Then you strum the muted chord.

Fig. 33A (Figs. 33A–33C will appear on audio track 15)

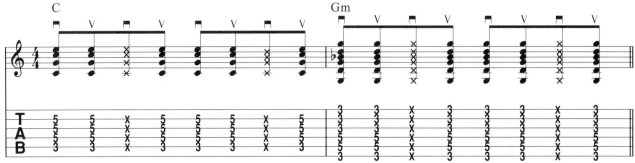

In Fig. 33B, we emphasize up-strokes as a way to get a unique sound. For each of the last three up-strokes in each measure, we play only the higher notes of the chord. Be sure, however, to hold the entire chord shape throughout the measure.

Fig. 33B

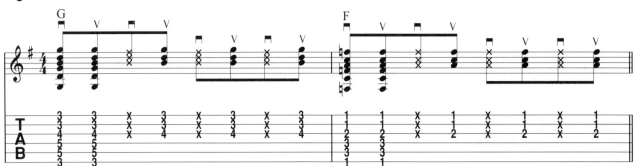

In Fig. 33C, you combine the above techniques. The lowest three notes are played with down-strokes, followed by muted notes with a down pick. The highest three notes are then an up-stroke.

Fig. 33C

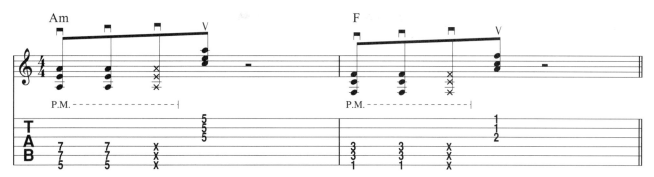

SOULFUL FILLS

Although they might sound intricate, the rhythm guitar parts featured in many R&B and soul classics are often based on simple fills closely related to common chord forms—usually barre chords with the root on the fifth or sixth string. We will base our riffs here on the popular I–IV progression. To give the chords a conventional funk or blues sound, we will use 7th and 9th chords. In the key of A, our sequence is A7 to D9. Fig. 34 is an A7 barre chord at the fifth fret with related fills, followed by a D9 at the fifth fret with a set of fills. As you play these licks, notice how each uses notes in and around the barre chord shape.

 Fig. 34 (Figs. 34 and 35 both appear on audio track 16)

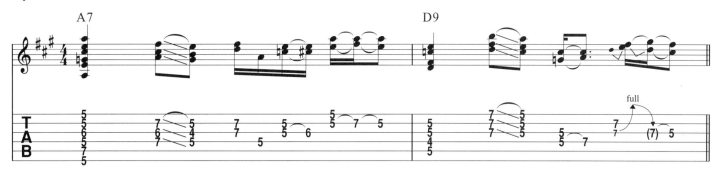

Fig. 35 is the same progression as Fig. 34, but played twice. This figure is a stripped-down version of Fig. 34—it leaves a lot more space by employing less notes, especially in measure 4.

Fig. 35

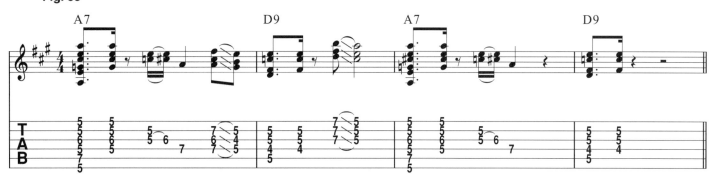

Fig. 36 employs another familiar progression: I–vi. Measures 1 and 2 are based on an A barre chord at the fifth fret, and the next two measures use an F#m form at the second fret. Again, note how each lick uses notes from the chord form. Since all these fills are based on movable chord forms, they are easily transposed to any key.

Because the A (A–C#–E) and F#m (F#–A–C#) chords have similar notes, you can use the fills inter-changably. Also, compare the fills for the A and the A7. Though you can often play A7 licks over an A chord (and A licks over an A7), in some progressions this exchange might not sound good—let your ear be the guide.

CHAPTER 2

FINGERPICKING

Even the most tired chord progressions can sound fresh when fingerpicking is used. If you are new to this technique, be patient—it will feel as if you're learning to use that hand for the first time. With a little practice, these patterns will soon seem like second nature.

The popular Am7–D (ii–V in G) sequence in Fig. 37 is composed of four one-measure exercises. Repeat each measure until you can play it evenly, with all the notes at a consistent volume, then move on to the next bar. Between the tab and standard notation are the symbols p, i, m and a. These represent the thumb (p), index (i), middle (m), and ring (a) fingers of the picking hand. When each section sounds and feels good, play the entire figure without any repeats.

 Fig. 37

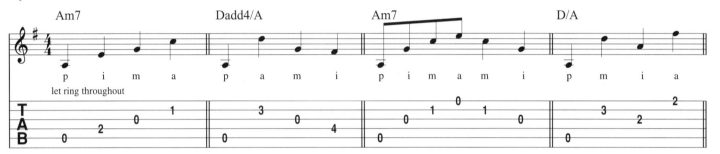

Fig. 38 builds upon the skills learned in Fig. 37. It also introduces the concept of *leading tones.* This technique involves step-wise resolution to a new note—evident here in beat 4 of measures 2 and 3.

Fig. 38

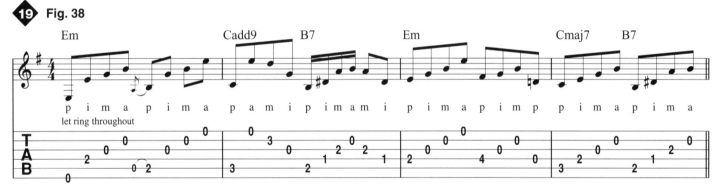

One of the best things about fingerpicking is that it gives you the ability to play non-adjacent strings simultaneously—something you can't do with a pick. Fig. 39 employs a standard pattern: the thumb and ring finger play the low and high notes respectively, while the index and middle fingers play the interior notes. This figure is built on a I–♭III–v–♭VII progression in A (A–C–Em–G). When a V chord appears in a progression, it is most often a dominant seventh chord (as in Fig. 38), but Fig. 39 employs a minor chord instead. Notice the different effect the minor chord creates.

 Fig. 39

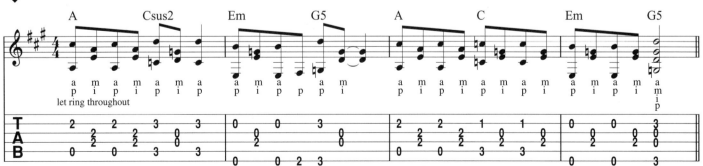

MORE FINGERPICKING

These figures introduce some new fingerpicking patterns and combine them with some of the previous examples.

Fig. 40 uses a two-measure pattern. Creating patterns like this that are less repetitive can keep your parts from sounding too predictable.

21 **Fig. 40**

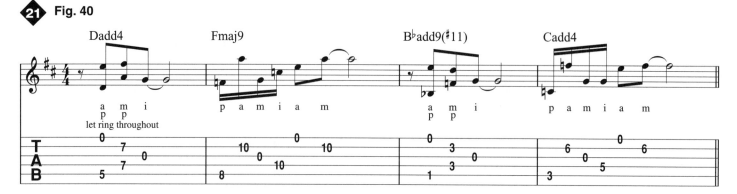

Fig. 41 employs a number of patterns; in fact, almost every measure is different.

22 **Fig. 41**

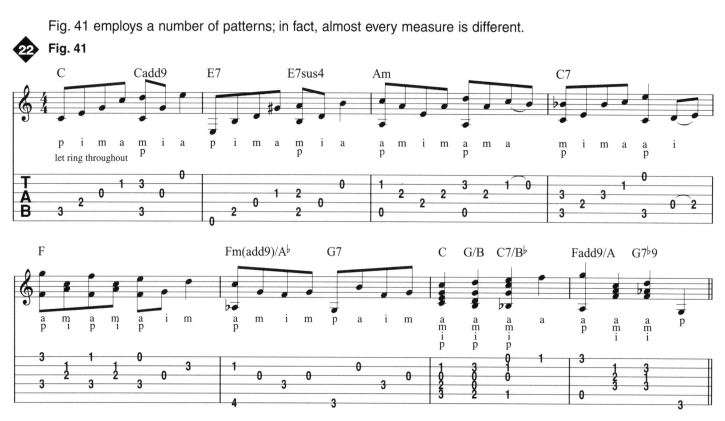

Typically, players use fingerpicking because it allows them to play non-adjacent notes simultaneously. However, sometimes you might want to use your fingers simply because they will give you a different sound. The Latin-style riff in Fig. 42, for example, could be played with a pick. But try it with fingers: play the single notes with your thumb and the chords with your first, second, and third fingers. Then play this figure with a pick so that you can hear the difference.

23 **Fig. 42**

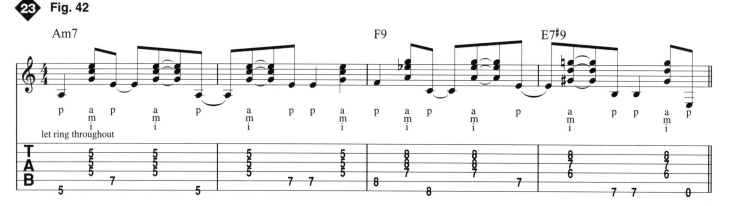

CHAPTER 3

EXPANDING YOUR HARMONIC VOCABULARY

Here we take a step back and look at the larger harmonic picture. We will focus on three basic chord qualities—major, minor, and dominant seventh—and explore the chords you can use as substitutes for each. With these substitutions, you can make even the simplest progression sound fresh and unique.

The chart in Fig. 43 lists six alternatives for each chord quality. This list is by no means exhaustive; it merely represents some of the more conventional and effective substitutes for the original chord. One note of caution: these substitutes will not work in all situations. Depending upon which key you are in, some of the alternative chords will work better than others—and some will sound just plain wrong. In general, the further you move down the substitution list, the greater the danger exists that the alternative chord may clash. And while the last few chords in each list might be perfect in a jazz setting, they might not fit in other situations. So experiment with all of the substitutes to see which ones sound best to you.

Fig. 43

For a major chord: sus2   sus4   add9   maj7   maj9   #11

Major substitutions

For a minor chord: sus2   sus4   m(add9)   m7   m9   m11

Minor substitutions

For a dominant seventh chord: 7sus2   7sus4   9   13   7#9   7#5

Dominant seventh substitutions

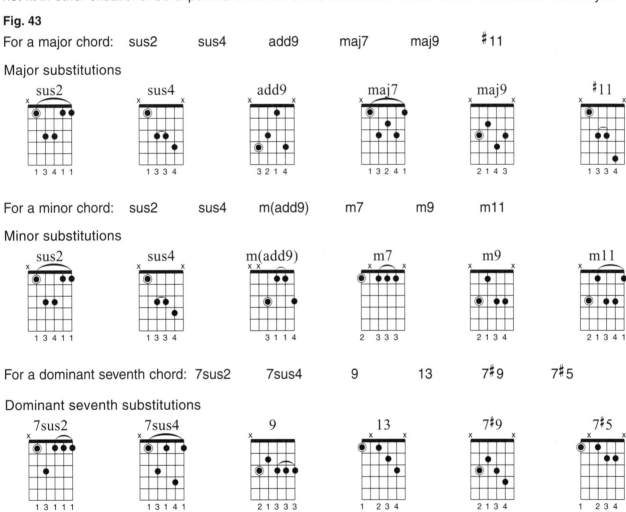

APPLYING YOUR EXPANDED HARMONIC VOCABULARY

The following figures illustrate some different ways that you can apply the ideas mentioned above. The first four bars of each figure comprise a typical chord progression. Underneath each progression is one example of how it could be modified by using the substitutions from Fig. 43. (Note: Although you can use substitutions in place of the original chord, you can also use them in addition to the original chord, as illustrated in Fig. 45.)

Fig. 44

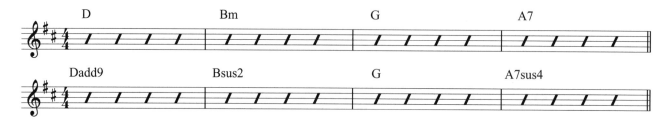

Fig. 45

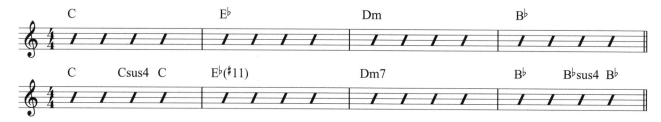

Fig. 46

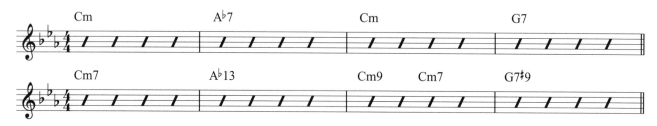

To make these progressions sound more exciting, play them with some of the techniques we explored elsewhere, such as the fingerpicking patterns from Chapter 2, or the strumming patterns from Chapter 1. If you need help in determining the proper fret at which to play each voicing, refer to the chart on page 5 (Fingerboard Note Names).

CHAPTER

12-BAR BLUES

The basis for untold numbers of blues, rock, jazz, and country tunes, the 12-bar blues is an extremely versatile, must-know progression. But which version?—Musicians play the progression in many different ways. Here and in the next section we cover the four most popular versions of the 12-bar blues.

Fig. 47 is the most basic style of the 12-bar blues—the version that rock 'n' roll guitar pioneer Chuck Berry often uses. In this figure, as in the others, the Roman numerals I, IV, and V identify the chord's relationship to the key. In the key of A, the I chord is A, the IV is D, and the V is E.

Fig. 47

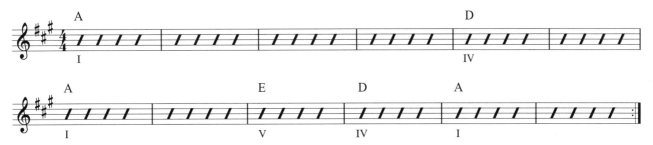

Fig. 48 is the version that most guitarists tend to employ. As we can see, all the chords have become 7th chords. The chords shown in parentheses, while not present in every version, are often used.

Fig. 48

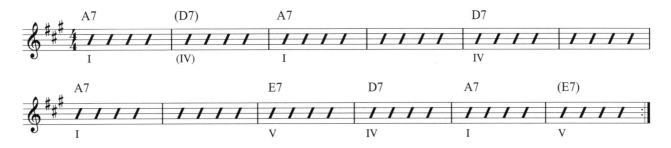

A typical rhythm guitar part for a 12-bar blues, Fig. 49 features the same one-measure riff transposed to each chord. Following the 12-bar chart above, simply play each riff over its respective chord and you have a typical 12-bar guitar part.

 Fig. 49 (Figs. 49–51 all appear an audio track 24)

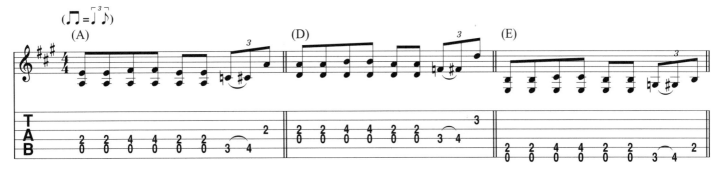

Figs. 50 and 51 demonstrate some other riffs that can be applied to the 12-bar progressions in Figs. 47 and 48. While these are not typical blues guitar parts, they help to illustrate the many possibilities that exist in the 12-bar format.

Fig. 50

Fig. 51

MORE 12-BAR BLUES

In Figs. 47 and 48, we looked at conventional versions of the 12-bar blues. Here we check out two more. For the sake of variety, however, these versions are in different keys. You can easily see the differences between each of these progressions by comparing the Roman numerals. The chords shown in parentheses are, again, substitutions which many players use. Refer to Fig. 52 for the chord voicings you'll need to know to play through the exercises in this Lesson. If you need help in determining the proper fret at which to play each voicing, refer to the chart on page 5.

Fig. 52

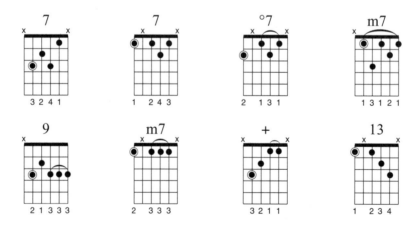

Fig. 53 is a 12-bar blues in the key of C. This version is commonly used by musicians who want more of a jazz sound. Compare the Roman numerals in measures 7–12 with those in measures 7–12 in Figs. 47 and 48 to hear how the changes give this version a jazz flavor.

Fig. 53

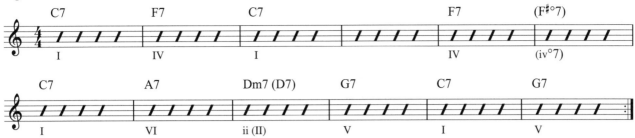

Fig. 54 includes three optional "turnarounds" that you could apply to Fig. 53. A *turnaround* is a series of chords at the end of a progression (almost always in the last two measures) which bring you back around to the beginning. You can use the two-measure turnarounds in this figure in place of measures 11–12 in Fig. 53.

Fig. 54

Fig. 55 is the most complicated version of the blues we'll explore. Keep in mind that all of these progressions can be modified by using the chord substitutions from Chapter 3.

Fig. 55

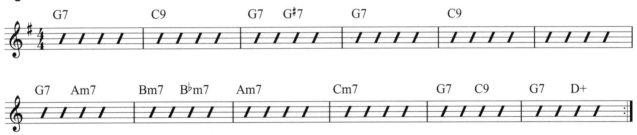

THE MINOR BLUES

Now let's examine the "minor blues." Relatively easy to play and memorize, the minor blues is an interesting alternative to the standard blues—and it's equally fun to solo over.

As we saw in Fig. 53, the standard blues is a 12-bar progression that uses three chords: I, IV, and V. These chords are usually played as major or 7th chords. The minor blues, also a 12-bar progression, generally uses four chords: i, iv, V, and ♭VI. Both progressions have I, IV, and V chords, but in the standard blues all the chords are major (or dominant). In the minor blues, however, the i and iv chords are minor and the V and ♭VI chords are usually major or 7th chords. (As the chord in parentheses in measure 9 of Fig. 56 shows, sometimes the ♭VI chord is played as a maj7.)

Fig. 56, a minor blues in the key of Am, features the progression in its most common form. If you want to play it with some different chords, try some of the substitutions from Chapter 3.

Fig. 56

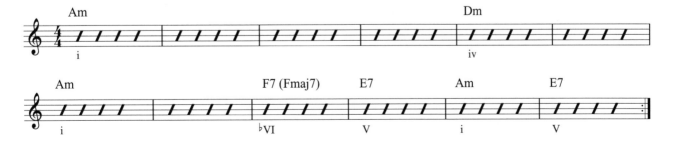

Fig. 57 demonstrates a possible guitar part based on the minor blues in Fig. 56. Notice how this part employs some substitutions: in measure 6 you play Dsus2 instead of Dm, and in measure 12 you play E7#9 in place of E7.

25 **Fig. 57**

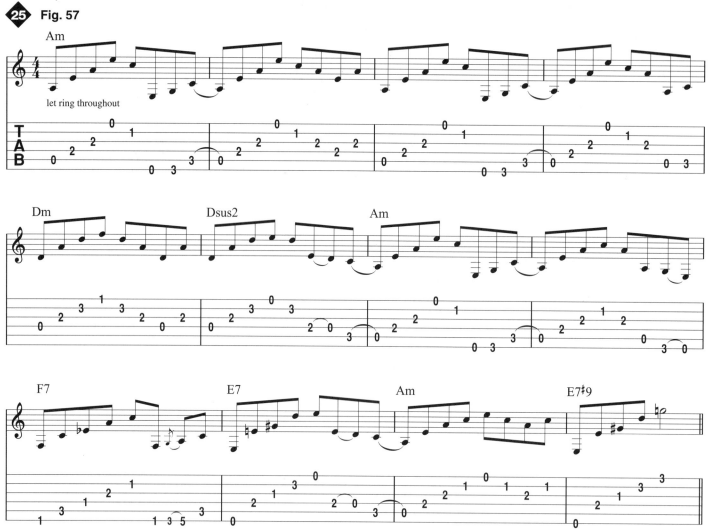

SOLOING OVER THE MINOR BLUES

As with any progression, the minor blues can be soloed over in a number of ways. Let's talk about three of them. First, we'll look at the most basic way: over each chord, you use the same scale—either an A minor pentatonic or an A blues. See Fig. 58A for some suggested patterns.

Fig. 58A

The second approach gets a little more complicated: In this case, a different scale is used for each chord. A minor pentatonic is used over the Am chord, D minor pentatonic for the Dm, A blues for the F7 chord, and A harmonic minor for the E7 (Fig. 58B). All the fingerings are in the same position so that you can easily switch between scales as the chords change. Over the F7, you can emphasize the blue note (♭5) in the A blues scale. This note, E♭, exists in the F7 chord (F–A–C–E♭) and is indicated in the diagram by a triangle.

Fig. 58B

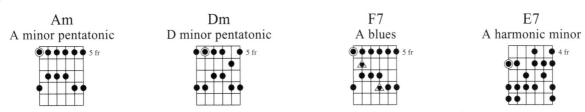

The third approach is the most involved because it uses modes and a hybrid scale. (For an explanation of the hybrid scales, see Chapter 14.) A Dorian is played over the Am chord, D Dorian over the Dm, F Mixolydian over the F7, and the A natural minor/harmonic minor hybrid scale over the E7. While some of the fingerings might not be familiar, once you get used to them, you'll find that they work great over these chords.

Fig. 58C

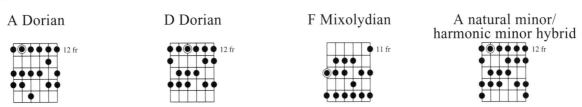

CHAPTER 5

ONE PROGRESSION—SEVEN RHYTHM GUITAR STYLES

In the following examples, we'll take a simple four-bar, four-chord progression (E–A–D–G) and play it in a number of different rhythm guitar styles: reggae, funk, country, etc. We will focus on the key aspects of each genre in order to see how the same progression can be played differently. When creating guitar parts, players often draw from whatever styles seem best for the tune; working with the seven figures on these pages should give you some new ideas for your own parts.

As you play each figure, notice what aspects are typical of each style: What kinds of chords does it use? Major? 7ths? 9ths? Where are the voicings played on the neck? On which strings? What type of strumming or picking pattern does it use? Is the style busy or sparse?

Soul/R&B:

 Fig. 59

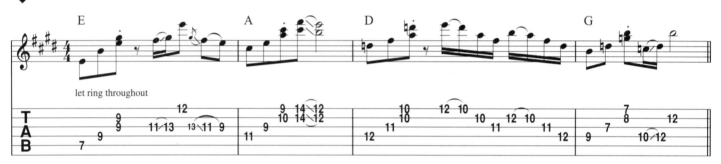

Funk:

 Fig. 60

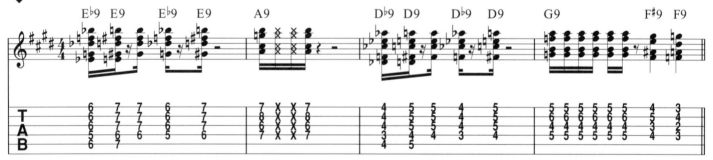

Country:

 Fig. 61

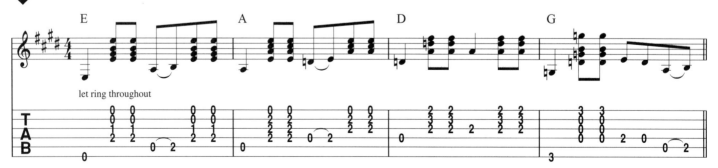

29 *Blues Shuffle:*

Fig. 62

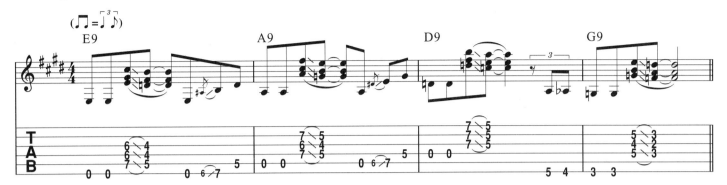

Reggae:

30 Fig. 63

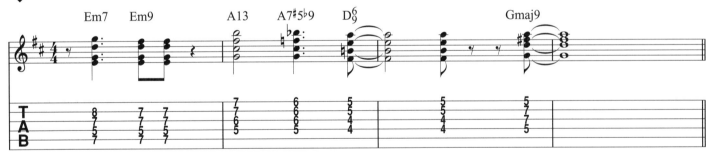

Since jazz progressions rarely use four consecutive major chords, I have kept the roots in this figure the same as in the others (E–A–D–G), but changed the qualities (Em7–A7–Dmaj7–Gmaj7) so that the progression becomes one that is commonly found in jazz standards. In this case, the chords form a typical ii–V–I–IV in D.

Jazz:

31 Fig. 64

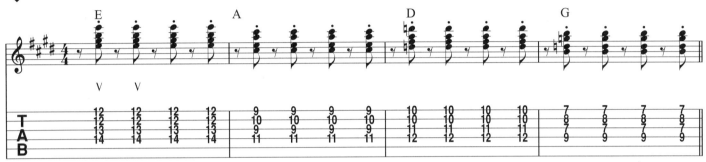

New Age:

32 Fig. 65

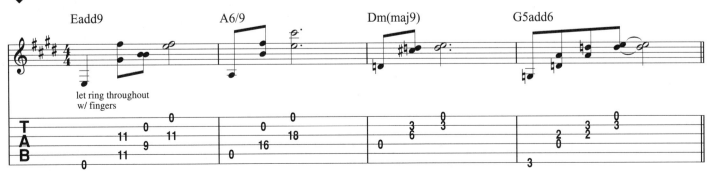

INVENTING PARTS FOR TWO GUITARS

Although a song can sometimes call for two guitars playing the same part, many times two very distinct parts will sound more interesting. In these cases, it is often best to emphasize contrast. For example, if one part consists of eighth-note strums, the other might employ sixteenth-note arpeggios. If one stays down low, the other could be up high. If one uses palm muting, the other doesn't.

Fig. 66 features highly contrasting guitar parts: Gtr. 1 plays a steady eighth-note riff with full voicings, while Gtr. 2 plays small voicings in a higher register. Since Gtr. 1 is relatively dense, Gtr. 2 plays a very simple part—one which leaves a lot of space. This way, the parts don't crowd each other.

 Fig. 66

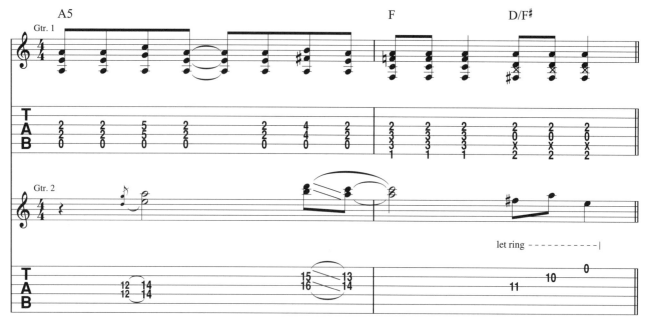

Notice how the chords in each part in Fig. 67 are slightly different. While Gtr. 1 arpeggiates Em(add9), Gtr. 2 plays Em and Em/G. When Gtr. 1 arpeggiates Dadd9, Gtr. 2 plays D/F♯ and D/A. By varying the chords in this manner, you can make the parts distinct, but keep them closely related.

 Fig. 67

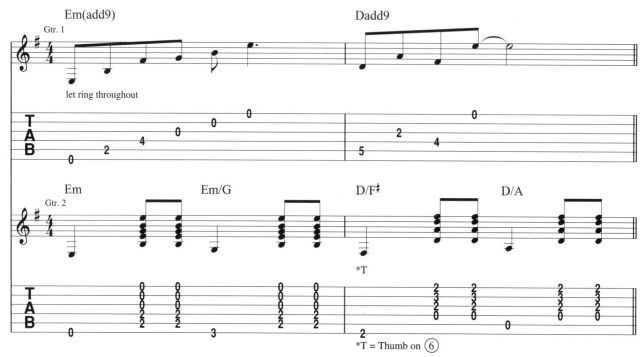

*T = Thumb on ⑥

In Fig. 68, the contrast is less dramatic. Both guitars make use of chords and often occupy the same register. However, because the parts are repetitive (especially Gtr. 2) and stay close to the harmony, they fit together well.

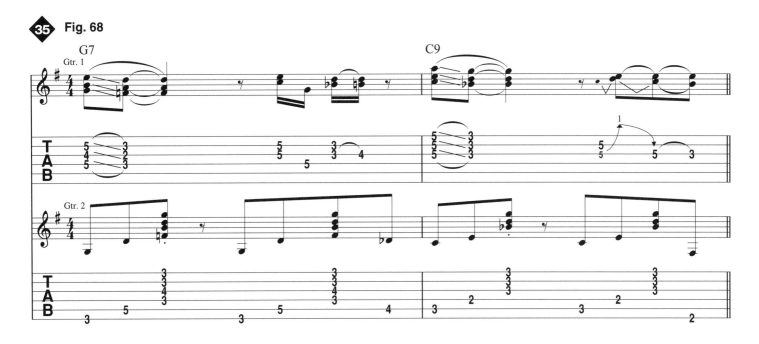

Studying transcriptions of tunes that use multiple guitar parts can be a great source of inspiration for your own writing. When creating parts, draw from the different styles in Figs. 59–65, as well as the chord substitution ideas in Chapter 3.

CLASSICAL GUITAR

Like learning to play any style of guitar, learning to play classical guitar is a full-time occupation. But the composition "Air" (Fig. 69) introduces you to a few fundamentals and gives you a simple but very musical solo piece to play. If you feel comfortable with the fingerpicking patterns in Chapter 2, you should be able to handle this piece without too much trouble. Classical pieces like "Air" typically require much more independence of motion, so plan on spending a little more time on this piece than you did on those patterns.

36 **Fig. 69**

CHAPTER 6

AGILITY DRILLS

As a way to both warm-up and work on technique, many players begin their practice sessions with agility drills. It's a good idea to start with simple drills and work your way up to more complex exercises. All of the figures in this lesson will help you build stamina, develop right- and left-hand coordination, and get your fingers moving in new ways.

Fig. 70 is a typical agility drill. It uses four consecutive notes on each string, starting from low to high. This drill is a good one to begin with because it is very symmetrical. It always uses the same order of fingers on the same frets—the only thing that changes is the string. (When you play these exercises make sure that you use strict alternate picking.)

Fig. 70

Fig. 71 gets a little more complicated. As you change strings, you also shift the direction of the notes. For example, the notes on the sixth string are ascending, while those on the fifth are descending. To execute the string changes smoothly, make your finger "roll over" to the next string. This creates a more seamless transition.

Fig. 71

Fig. 72 breaks up the order of the notes—instead of 1–2–3–4, on each string, we now have 1–4–3–2 on one string and 1–4–2–3 on the next. We also shift direction, starting on string 1 and work our way down to string 6.

Fig. 72

Fig. 73 is particularly helpful in developing coordination between your hands.

Fig. 73

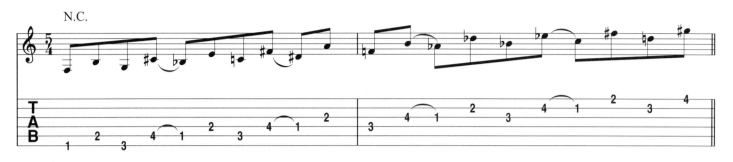

Most of these drills start from the lowest string and move to the highest. After you get each drill down this way, try playing it from string 1 down to string 6 (as we did in Fig. 72).

CHAPTER 7

PENTATONIC SCALES AND VARIATIONS

It's safe to say that pentatonic scales are the harmonic basis for most rock and pop guitar solos. Even though there are a lot of useful fingerings, some players tend to employ only one or two. So here we will look at many different fingerings of the two main types—major and minor pentatonic—and some interesting variations.

All of the fingering in Figs. 74A–D have the root on the 6th string. Fig. 74A is a basic minor pentatonic fingering. Fig. 74B is the blues scale—the minor pentatonic with an added ♭5 note (also called the "blue note"). The note indicated by a triangle is a chromatic passing note. While this note is technically not part of the blues scale, I have included it as an option because players often use it. When you practice this scale, play it with and without this note. Fig. 74C features an added ninth. This subtle variation of the minor pentatonic scale is often referred to as a "hexatonic" scale. Fig. 74D is a three-notes-per-string hybrid version of all three scales.

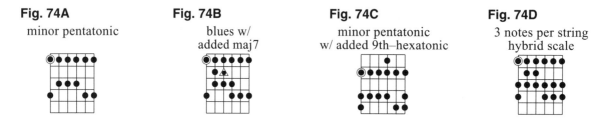

Fig. 74A
minor pentatonic

Fig. 74B
blues w/
added maj7

Fig. 74C
minor pentatonic
w/ added 9th–hexatonic

Fig. 74D
3 notes per string
hybrid scale

Figs. 75A–D features the same types of scales as Fig. 74, but the root of each fingering pattern is on the fifth string.

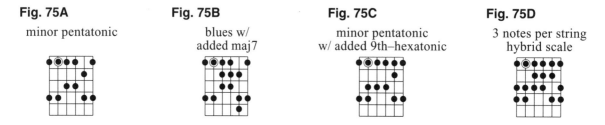

Fig. 75A
minor pentatonic

Fig. 75B
blues w/
added maj7

Fig. 75C
minor pentatonic
w/ added 9th–hexatonic

Fig. 75D
3 notes per string
hybrid scale

Figs. 76A and 76B contain fingerings of the minor pentatonic that move up the neck, as opposed to those in Figs. 74 and 75 which stay in one position. These scales give you a far greater range of notes than single-position scales.

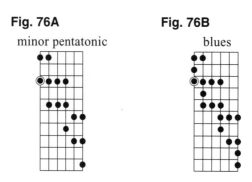

Fig. 76A
minor pentatonic

Fig. 76B
blues

The fingerings in Fig. 77A and 77B have the root on the fifth string.

Fig. 77A   **Fig. 77B**

minor pentatonic   blues

MINOR-MAJOR PENTATONIC CONVERSION

The fingerings in Figs. 74A, 75A, 76A, and 77A can function as both minor and major pentatonic scales. The root note (the circled note in each of these diagrams) indicates the tonic of the scale if you are thinking of it as a minor pentatonic. So, if you are playing Fig. 74A at the 1st fret, this scale is F minor pentatonic (F–A♭–B♭–C–E♭). A glance at the conversion chart (Fig. 78) tells you that this scale contains the same notes as the A♭ major pentatonic (A♭–B♭–C–E♭–F). If you are playing over a chord progression (let's say C to B♭) and know that you want to use the C major pentatonic (C–D–E–G–A), you can see from the conversion chart that it's the same as A minor pentatonic (A–C–D–E–G). Therefore, you can use the A minor pentatonic fingerings and licks that you are familiar with.

Fig. 78

Minor	E	A	D	G	C	F	B♭	E♭	A♭(G♯)	D♭(C♯)	F♯	B
Major	G	C	F	B♭	E♭	A♭	D♭	G♭	C♭(B)	F♭(E)	A	D

PENTATONIC LICKS

The figures here give you some idea of the kinds of licks you can create using the scales from the previous examples.

Fig. 79 uses the D minor hexatonic fingering from Fig. 74C.

 Fig. 79

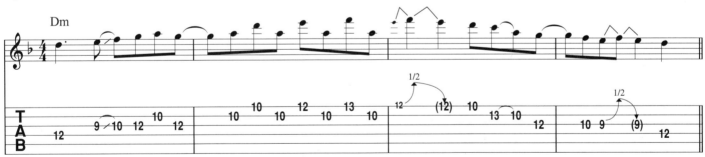

The lick in Fig. 80 is based on the fingering in Fig. 74B. It uses the A blues scale with the chromatic passing note. There are two ways to think of and use this lick: as an A blues lick or a C major pentatonic lick with some passing tones—similar to what you might hear in a southern or country rock setting. The chromatic notes from the related minor scale (see the chart in Fig. 78) add some extra flavor.

38 **Fig. 80**

Fig. 81 is based on the three-notes-per-string hybrid scale fingering (Fig. 74D).

39 **Fig. 81**

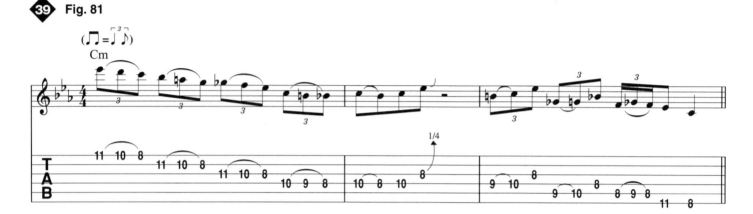

While players often stay in one position when soloing, it's a good idea to build licks that shift position and/or use variations of the minor pentatonic scale. Fig. 82, for example, combines three fingerings. Measure 1 is based on the minor pentatonic scale in Fig. 76A. In measure 2, the lick shifts positions to the hexatonic fingering from Fig. 75C. The final measure stays in the same position and uses notes from the blues scale with a chromatic passing note (Fig. 75B).

40 **Fig. 82**

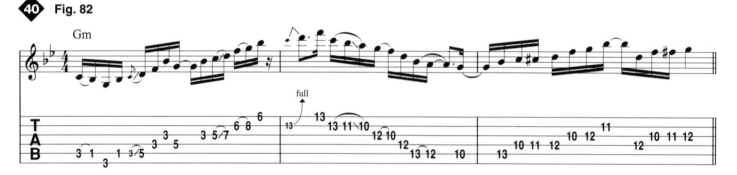

BENDING

Players often get in a rut of bending the same few notes in a scale the same distance. In the E minor pentatonic at the 12th fret (Fig. 83), for example, there are three common whole-step bends: the A to B (14th fret, third string); D to E (15th fret, 2nd string); G to A (15th fret, 1st string).

41 **Fig. 83**

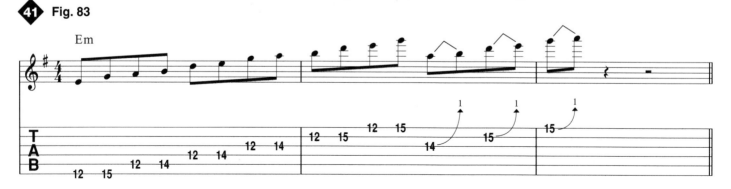

Fig. 84 shows that within the same fingering there are a number of other notes you can bend. At first, you might find it difficult to play some of the first-finger bends in this figure. When players bend notes with the third or fourth finger, they often use the other fingers to help push the string. Since there is no possibility of such additional support with a first finger bend, it might take a while to build up the necessary strength. When bending with this finger (as with any finger), you usually have two choices: you can either bend the note towards you (up) or away from you (down). The direction you choose will depend in part on which string you are on. Experiment with both directions to see which way feels most comfortable on each string.

42 Fig. 84

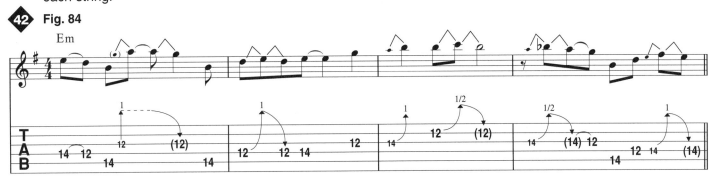

Players tend to only bend notes on the three highest strings; they are the lightest and therefore bend the easiest. But this leaves a large part of the guitar's range unused for bending. The D Mixolydian (D–E–F♯–G–A–B–C) lick in Fig. 85 uses half- and whole-step bends on the fourth and fifth strings. While bends on these strings can be difficult, adding a few to your repertoire will dramatically increase your bending options within a scale fingering.

43 Fig. 85

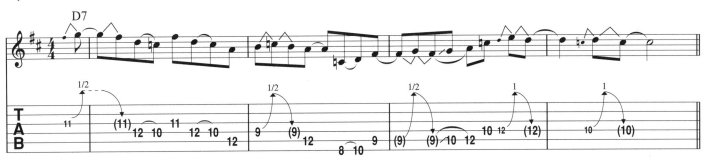

The A7 lick in Fig. 86 uses notes from both the A minor pentatonic (A–C–D–E–G) and A major pentatonic scales (A–B–C♯–E–F♯). This figure also features an easy half-step bend as well as some difficult bends: a one and half-step bend, and a bend that involves two consecutive whole steps.

44 Fig. 86

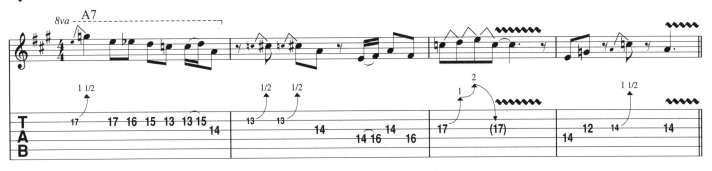

CHAPTER 8

BENDING WITH DYADS AND TRIADS

When it comes to bends that involve two notes, many players have a few favorites, such as those in Fig. 87. In Figs. 88–90, we will usually bend only one note of the dyad or triad at a time, but as we will find in Fig. 88, you can also bend two notes simultaneously.

45 **Fig. 87**

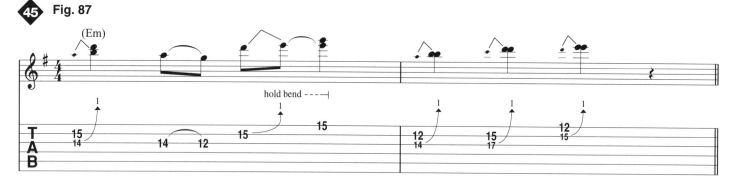

The C7 licks in Fig. 88 are typical of the bends we will look at. In measure 1, the lower note is bent up a half step. It can be hard to bend one note without bending the other, but this will come with practice. Because the bend in measure 2 involves two notes on the same fret, you could play both notes with the same finger. But also try bending the low note with your third finger and the high note with your fourth. When you use two fingers, you have more strength and control than when using only one.

46 **Fig. 88**

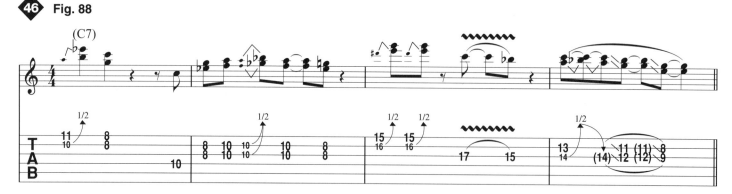

Fig. 89 is based on D Mixolydian (D–E–F♯–G–A–B–C). The trickiest part of this lick lies in measures 2 and 3. Here, you must bend the first note the appropriate distance, then, while holding the bend, play the note on the first string. While that note is still ringing, release the bent note back to its original pitch. For the final bend in this figure, bend the note on the ninth fret with your ring finger while playing the two notes on the tenth fret with your pinky.

47 **Fig. 89**

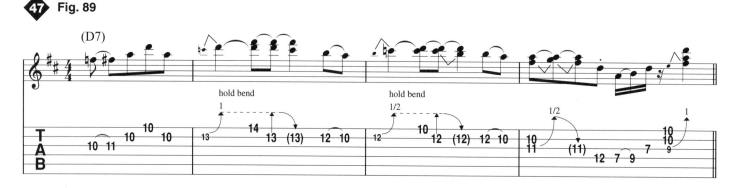

In Fig. 90, we bend the highest note in each arpeggio a half step. In measures 1 and 2, you should hold the first finger down until you need to use it for the bend. Let the notes that fall under your third and fourth fingers ring throughout the entire measure. The first-finger bends in this figure can be difficult, but the pedal steel-like effect you'll achieve will make it worth the effort.

48 Fig. 90

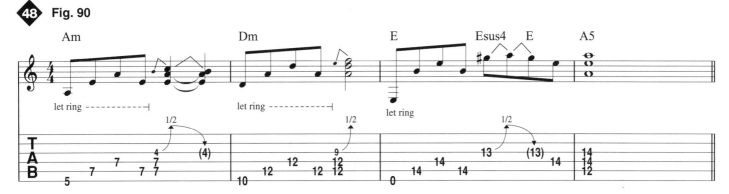

SIXTHS

When soloing, sixths offer an alternative to single notes and conventional doublestop licks. The two notes that form the sixth are usually played on non-adjacent strings, and there may be some difficulty in deciding how to finger them. If the two notes are on the same fret, you could use a barre or a combination of fingers—index and middle, middle and ring, or ring and pinky. If the notes are not on the same fret, you could conceivably use any of these three combinations. So it might take you a while to determine which fingering is best. Feel free to experiment with different combinations as you work through the following examples.

Fig. 91A features an A7 chord followed by a series of sixths that stay relatively close to the chord form. The sixths in Fig. 91B, however, are all played on the same two strings: the first and third. These sixths are derived from an A Mixolydian scale (A–B–C♯–D–E–F♯–G) and work well over an A7 chord. Pluck the sixths in both figures with your fingers (or use a pick for the low note and the middle finger for the high note). Fig. 91C is a typical A7 lick using the sixths from Fig. 91A. Fig. 91D is an A7 lick based on Fig. 91B. Try these figures with and without a pick.

49 Fig. 91A (Figs. 91A–91D all appear on audio track 49)

Fig. 91B A7

Fig. 91C

Fig. 91D

The sixths in Figs. 92A-92D are based on the A Dorian scale (A–B–C–D–E–F#–G). Fig. 92A contains an Am7 chord followed by sixths that stay near the chord form, while the sixths in Fig. 92B move up the neck. Fig. 92C is an Am7 lick using the sixths from Fig. 92A, while Fig. 92D uses licks derived from Fig. 92B in measure 1, and licks from Fig. 91B (transposed to fit over a D7 chord) in measure 2.

50 **Fig. 92A** (Figs. 92A–92B both appear on audio track 50)

Am7

Fig. 92B

Am7

51 **Fig. 92C** (Figs. 92C–92D both appear on audio track 51)

Am7

Fig. 92D

Am7   D7

let ring   let ring

Figs. 93A and 93B show two scales harmonized in sixths on the third and first strings. Fig. 93A is based on an F major scale, and Fig. 93B is based on an F natural minor scale. The fret with a circle indicates the root of the scale. Try using this approach in any situation where you would normally use the conventional single-note form of the scale. For example, if you solo over a progression with G natural minor, use Fig. 93B starting at the third fret.

Fig. 93A
F major scale

Fig. 93B
F minor scale

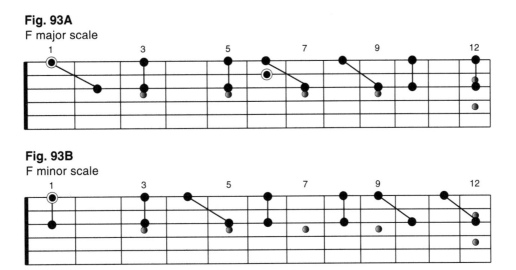

CHAPTER

TRIAD ARPEGGIOS

In addition to scales and sixths (see Chapter 8), we need to explore arpeggios—the notes of a chord played as a series of single notes. In this chapter, we will learn arpeggios in small groups of three or four notes played on two or three strings. Although any chord could be arpeggiated across all six strings, such arpeggios are a bit cumbersome and therefore difficult to use in soloing. So most players tend to use smaller versions like those in Figs. 94–96.

Fig. 94 features major triad arpeggios in root position. Beginning with G major, we progress through a series of 4ths until we reach E♭.

Fig. 94

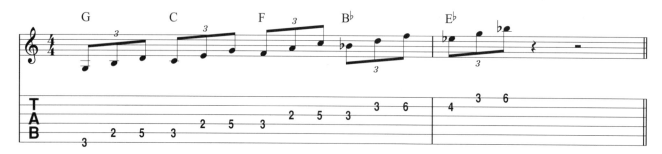

Fig. 95 shows the minor versions of the arpeggios in Fig. 94.

Fig. 95

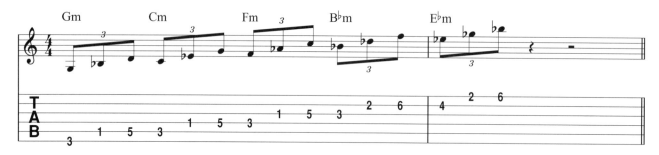

All the arpeggios in Figs. 94 and 95 are in root position. This simply means that the lowest note is the root of the arpeggio. Fig. 96 shows some other common three- and four-note arpeggios, but they are inverted (not in root position). The circled note in the tablature and standard notation indicates the root.

Fig. 96

Fig. 97 is a series of triad arpeggios based on the notes in a G minor pentatonic scale (G–B♭–C–D–F). The arpeggios are: Gm (G–B♭–D), B♭ (B♭–D–F), C (C–E–G), Dm (D–F–A), and F (F–A–C). The tones E and A are borrowed from the G Dorian scale. This figure will work in most situations where you would use a G minor pentatonic scale.

52 **Fig. 97**

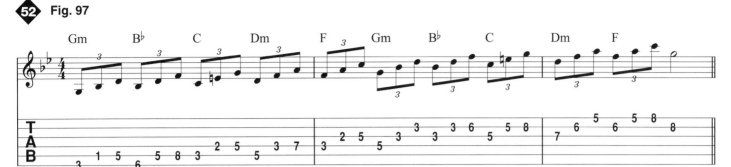

MORE TRIAD ARPEGGIOS

Figs. 98–101 use the arpeggios from Figs. 94–96. Each figure here has a chord in parentheses written above the key signature. This will tell you what chord(s) these licks will fit over. The chord names in brackets represent the names of each arpeggio.

53 **Figs. 98**

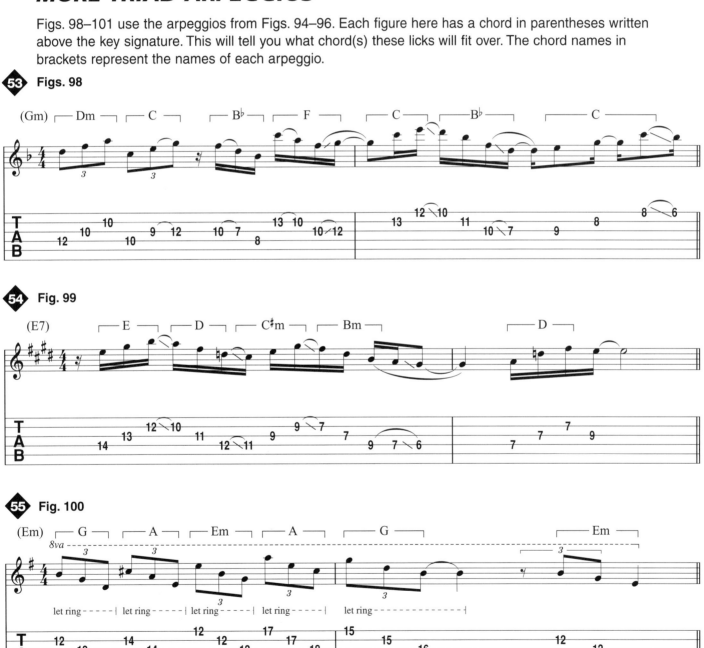

54 **Fig. 99**

55 **Fig. 100**

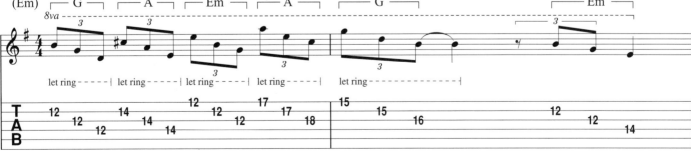

Fig. 101

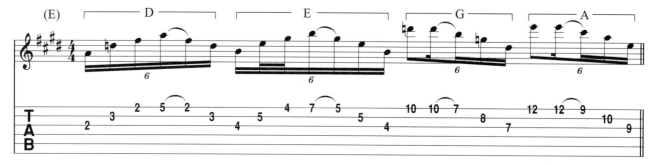

Notice how the licks in Figs. 98–101 create some variety by shifting the direction of the arpeggios and by using slides and slurs. One of the major difficulties that arises when playing arpeggios is determining how to pick them: should you use strict alternate picking (down-up-down-up), or some other picking pattern? This is normally best left up to the individual. Experiment with several methods to determine which one suits you.

CHAPTER 10

SOLOING WITH ONE SCALE PER CHORD

Many times when soloing, guitarists often only use one scale for the entire progression. However, because there are usually a number of scales that will work over any chord, a simple four-chord progression might yield dozens of scale combinations you could use. While you are soloing, though, it's difficult to keep a lot of information in your head about which chord gets what scale. So here's an easy formula that will work in most situations:

- For a major chord: play the major pentatonic starting from the root.

- For a minor chord: play the minor pentatonic or blues scale starting from the root.

- For a 7th chord: play the major pentatonic or the minor/major pentatonic hybrid starting from the root (see Chapter 14—Hybrid Scales).

Fig. 102 features the progression C–Em–B♭–G7 (I–iii–♭VII–V in C). Underneath each chord is a corresponding fingering derived from the above formula. (For other fingerings of these pentatonic scales, see Chapters 4, 7, and 14.)

Fig. 102

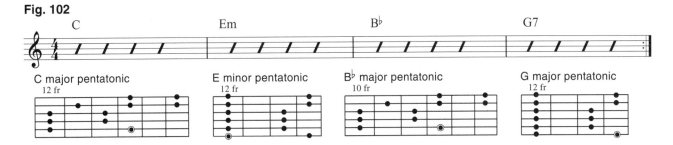

Fig. 103 is a ii–V in G major. This progression differs slightly from Fig. 102 in that the chords here are m7 and 9th chords rather than triads. But as we learned in Chapter 3 [Expanding Your Harmonic Vocabulary], the m7 chord is a common substitution for a minor chord and a 9th chord is a common substitution for a 7th chord. So we can think of the Am7 (A–C–E–G) as an Am and use the scales our chord/scale formula suggests. And similarly, because the 9th chord is a substitution for the 7th, over the D9 (D–F♯–A–C–E) we can use the scales that the formula recommends for a 7th chord. So below each chord are two fingerings derived from the formula. The boxes in the hybrid scale identify the notes in a D9, the notes that players often emphasize when soloing over this chord.

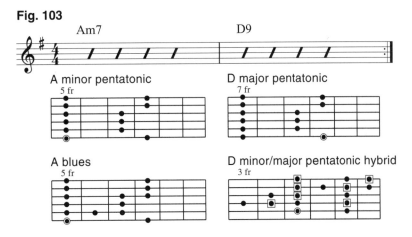

Fig. 103

Try applying the formula when improvising over other progressions, such as those in Chapter 3 [Applying Your Expanded Harmonic Vocabulary]. You'll be surprised at how easy this formula is to use and how nice it sounds.

SOLOING OVER A MINOR CHORD

Let say that you're playing a solo over a Dm chord. The default choice for most players is the D minor pentatonic scale (D–F–G–A–C) or the D blues scale (D–F–G–A♭–A–C). While these scales work well, there are many other scales that you could use, scales that will give your solos a different sound. Three possible scales are the D natural minor scale (D–E–F–G–A–B♭–C), the D Dorian scale (D–E–F–G–A–B–C), and the D harmonic minor scale (D–E–F–G–A–B♭–C♯). The D Phrygian scale (D–E♭–F–G–A–B♭–C) may also work, though it sounds a little less conventional than some of the others. Check out Fig. 104 for two suggested fingerings of each of the above scales.

Fig. 104

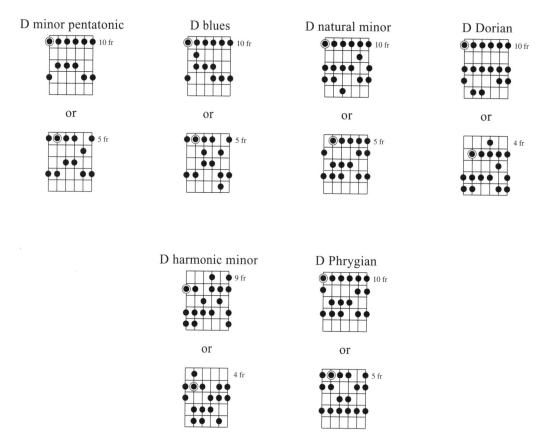

When soloing over a minor chord, you can also use the minor pentatonic based on the 5th of the chord. In the case of a Dm chord (D–F–A), the 5th is A. So you could use an A minor pentatonic over a Dm chord. An easy way to determine the fifth of any chord is to play that chord as a two-note power chord. The fifth is the note under your third finger.

But don't think of these scales as an either/or choice. A skilled player can move in and out of different scales effortlessly. While soloing over a Dm chord, you could move back and forth between the D and A minor pentatonic. You might start with some of your favorite pentatonic licks, then move into the D Dorian mode, and end with a flurry of notes from D harmonic minor. Fig. 104 shows these scales in two positions (the tenth and fifth) so that it's easy for you to move between them.

As I mentioned, the D Dorian scale will work. And because this scale contains the same notes as the C major scale (C–D–E–F–G–A–B), you can use any C major fingerings, licks, patterns, or sequences that you know (see Chapter 12 for sequencing ideas). Since we know that the notes of a C major scale will fit, we can use other material from the key of C, such as arpeggios built on notes in the C major scale—these would be C, Dm, Em, F, G, Am, and B°. Ultimately, scales are simply the starting places for finding material to use.

CHAPTER 11

STRING SKIPS

We as guitarists sometimes tend to play in a very scalar fashion. After playing notes on the third string, for instance, we will move either to the second string or the fourth. Consequently, our soloing can sometimes sound as if we are just running up and down scales. You can break this habit by using "string skips." In the first measure of Fig. 105, for example, the first two notes are played on the sixth string. Then you skip over the fifth string and play notes on the fourth.

Fig. 105

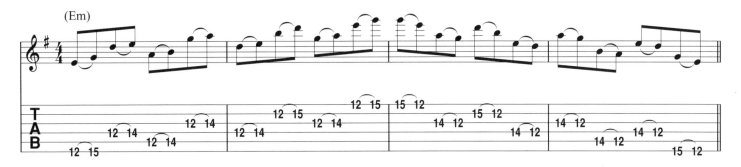

Since it's a good idea to start practicing string skips on a familiar scale, Fig. 105 employs a standard fingering of the E minor pentatonic scale (E–G–A–B–D). First play the figure as written, with slurs. When you feel confident this way, try picking each note. This method will be more difficult because it requires you to move your picking hand faster. So start at a slow tempo and gradually speed up. Try the following figures with and without slurs as well.

Fig. 106 uses the same fingering as Fig. 105, but here we use the D minor pentatonic scale (D–F–G–A–C).

57 **Fig. 106**

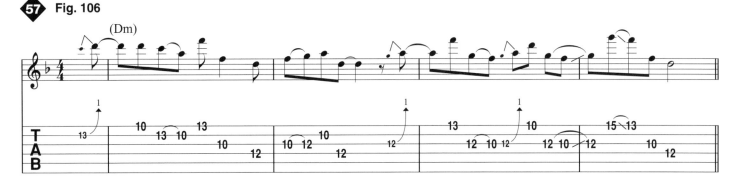

While most of the lick in Fig. 107 is in one position, it also shifts position twice. These kinds of shifts will give you the large intervals that string skips provide.

58 **Fig. 107**

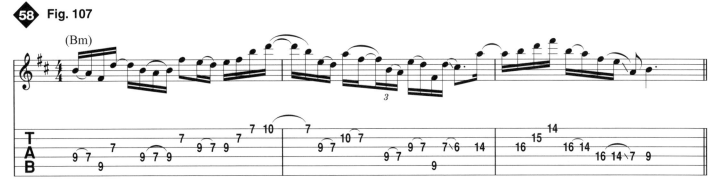

Although we have used the minor pentatonic scale as the basis for these three figures, you can use string skips on any kind of scale. So be sure to practice this technique with any major or minor scales that you know.

OPEN-STRING LICKS

When you play a lick or a riff, you usually don't want the notes to blend into each other. But the figures here have a unique sound created by unusual combinations of fretted and open notes ringing together. This technique, used often in country guitar, can add a fresh sound to an otherwise ordinary line.

Even though Fig. 108 could be played with all fretted notes in one position, we will use open strings and position shift in order to allow the notes to ring together. In measure 1, for example, the first, second, and third notes ring together. You then play the fourth note by taking your finger off the second string, being careful to let the other notes continue to ring. Then the fifth and sixth notes should ring together (you will need to shift out of third position here). Make sure that you let the open first, second, and third strings continue to ring after they have been played; all these notes blending together give you a harp-like effect that is extremely difficult to get with only fretted notes.

 Fig. 108

Figs. 109 and 110 use open notes in typical country-rock style licks. While in Fig. 108, we wanted as many fretted and open notes to ring together as possible, in these figures we only want some of the open notes to ring. So pay careful attention to the "let ring" notation in the tablature. The lick in Fig. 109 is based on a G7 (G–B–D–F). You could play this lick as one phrase, or you could think of each measure as a short lick.

 Fig. 109

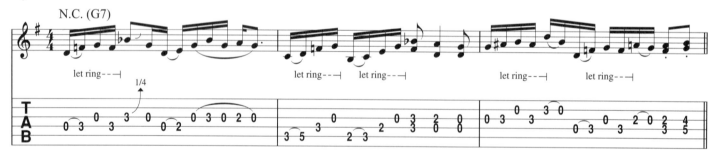

 Fig. 110

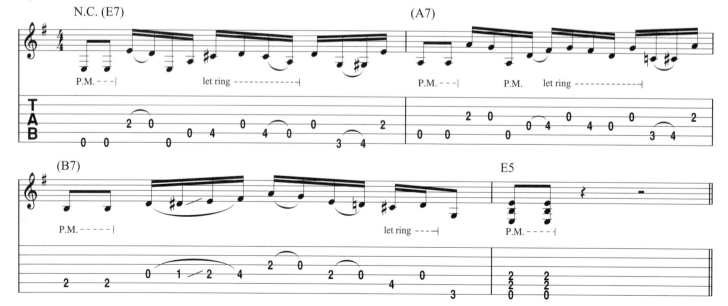

SEQUENCES

A sequence is simply any pattern that repeats. Guitar players often use sequences as sources for solo licks and as exercises for warming-up. As you are learning the following figures, pick each note and use strict alternate picking. Once you have them under your fingers, then play them as written (with the hammer-ons and pull-offs).

The sequence in Fig. 111 is based upon a G major scale (G–A–B–C–D–E–F#). To calculate a sequence, we first need to assign a number to each note. Since players typically refer to the notes in a scale by their number, we will use the conventional numbers: G=1, A=2, B=3, etc. A typical number sequence is 1,2,3,4 — 2,3,4,5 — 3,4,5,6 — 4,5,6,7, etc. As notes in a G major scale, this translates to G,A,B,C — A,B,C,D — B,C,D,E — C,D,E,F#, etc. Fig. 111 takes this sequence through a ninth-position G major scale.

Fig. 111

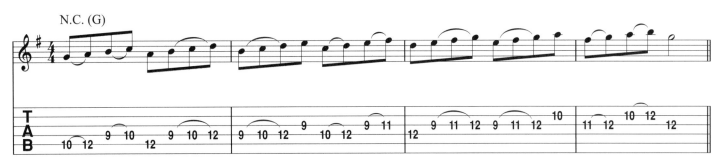

Another common sequence is 1,3 — 2,4 — 3,5 — 4,6 — etc. In Fig. 112, we play this sequence in a tenth-position C natural minor scale, going from the root to the highest note and then back down to the root. You will likely find going down a little more difficult.

62 **Fig. 112**

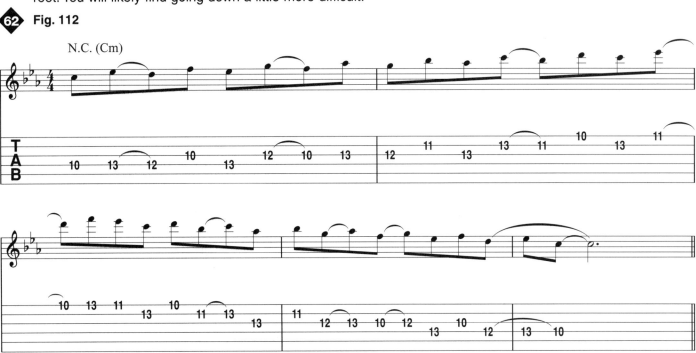

Fig. 113 uses the sequence from Fig. 111, but this time we use an A minor pentatonic scale
(A–C–D–E–G).

Fig. 113

After you get comfortable with these sequences, apply them to other scale fingerings that you know. If
you try them on the hybrid scales found in Chapter 14, they will yield some pretty unconventional patterns which are hard to play but sound great.

MORE SEQUENCES

As with Figs. 111–113, play the following figures first by picking every note (use strict alternate picking)
and then as written with slurs.

Based upon a D natural minor scale (D–E–F–G–A–B♭–C), Fig. 114 uses a sequence that is eight notes
long: 1,2,3,4,5,4,3,2 — 3,4,5,6,7,6,5,4,— 5,6,7,8,9,8,7,6 — etc. Towards the end of the figure, though, we
move out of the sequence and into some bends. It's often a good idea to disrupt the pattern after a cou-
ple of repetitions to avoid becoming stale or predictable.

 Fig. 114

The sequence in Fig. 115 uses a three-note-per-string D major scale (D–E–F♯–G–A–B–C♯). It's probably
easiest to finger this scale using your first, second, and fourth fingers for the three notes on every string.

 Fig. 115

Figs.116 and 117 take a slightly looser approach to the idea of sequences. Unlike the other sequences
we have looked at, these do not consistently follow the pattern. Both figures also involve a *pivot* note—a
note that the lick constantly returns to. In Fig. 116, the pivot note is always the open first string. In Fig.
117, however, the pivot note changes. In the first measure it is the G note (fifth fret, fourth string). But
throughout the rest of the figure, the pivot shifts to other notes in the G minor pentatonic scale
(G–B♭–C–D–F) that the sequence is based upon.

65 **Fig. 116**

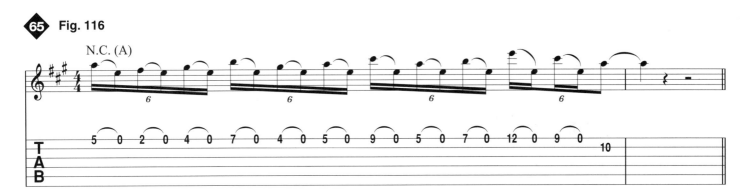

66 **Fig. 117**

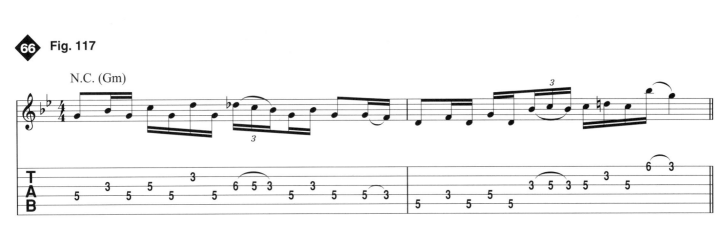

Try creating your own sequences. At first, it may be a bit difficult. However, you will find that sequences are not only excellent for developing technique (many times they will force you to use all four fingers of your fretting hand), but they may also bring you into previously unexplored realms of the fretboard.

CHAPTER 13

MELODIC INTERVALS

Our phrasing can sound predictable and uninteresting when we solo with only a limited number of intervals (an interval is the distance between two notes). When moving from note to note within a scale, we often play the note immediately above or below the one we just played. This means that we end up employing rather small intervals, such as a minor 2nd (a half step, or one fret), a major 2nd (a whole step, or two frets), or a minor 3rd (one and a half steps, or three frets). We addressed this issue previously with string skips, and now we'll look at another method to avoid this.

Measure 1 in Fig. 118 is partially based on the interval of a perfect fifth. The distance between the first and second notes (D and A), as well as between the second and third notes (A and E), is a perfect 5th. The measure ends with another 5th, (A to E) played one octave higher. The long slides and the position shifts in the lick also give you some atypical intervals (4ths, 5ths, major 7ths, and minor 7ths).

 Fig. 118

Fig. 119 is based on the E natural minor scale (E–F#–G–A–B–C–D). The brackets over the notes in this figure indicate the sequence and its two repetitions. (For information about sequences, see Chapter 12). When you play these kinds of sequences, you can often end up with some larger intervals: the distance from the last note in each bracket to the first note in the next bracket, for example, is a minor 6th.

 Fig. 119

Fig. 119 features a linear scale pattern—one which moves up or down (rather than across) the fingerboard and is played on a limited number of strings. Because it's easy to use slides when you move these fingerings through each position (as we do at the ends of each sequence in the figure), these kinds of scale patterns can give your playing a smooth and connected sound.

Like Fig. 119, Fig. 120 uses a sequence of repeating intervals (here a 4th followed by two 2nds), and we play inversions of the sequence as well. (A sequence is inverted by playing the notes in the reverse order.) The notes in bracket 1 (G–C–D–E♭) reappear one octave higher in bracket 1a; but this time they are inverted (E♭–D–C–G). The notes in bracket 2a invert the notes in bracket 2 as well. This figure is a kind of catalog of intervals: it uses 2nds, 3rds, 4ths, 5ths, 6ths, and 7ths.

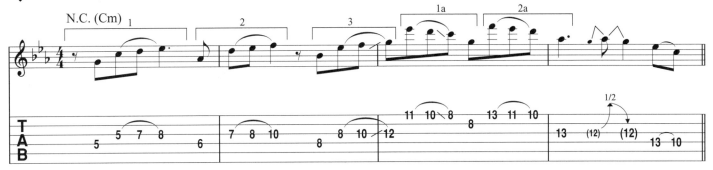

IMPROVISING WITH CHROMATIC NOTES

A chromatic note is simply any note that isn't part of the key you are playing in. Because chromatic notes are outside the harmony, you can use them to add some color and harmonic tension to your phrases. The only thing to be careful of is emphasis: skilled players tend to avoid staying too long on them. Instead, soloists often use chromatic notes as passing notes—notes in between two consecutive scale notes, or approach notes—notes a half-step below or above a chord or scale tone.

The following figures use common scales (minor pentatonic, Mixolydian, Dorian) combined with chromatic notes (indicated by *). After you have worked on these figures, try making up new licks using the chromatic notes available around other fingerings that you know.

Fig. 121 employs the A Dorian scale (A–B–C–D–E–F♯–G) and a few of the many possible chromatic notes around the scale in this position. Notice how some of the chromatic notes are used as passing notes and others as approach notes.

70 Fig. 121

The G Mixolydian scale (G–A–B–C–D–E–F) is the source for Fig. 122. Since this scale is closely associated with the G7 chord (G–B–D–F), this lick can be used when soloing over a G7.

71 Fig. 122

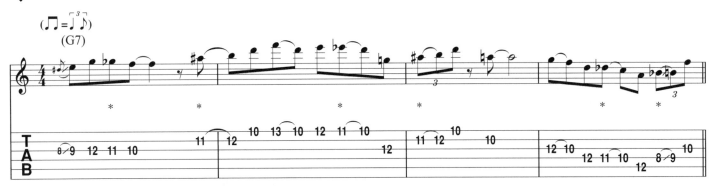

Another way to incorporate chromaticism into your playing is by shifting a diatonic pattern up or down one or more frets. This idea is the basis for the chromatic notes in the G minor lick in Fig. 123. The notes under bracket 1 form a pattern that you move to two other frets (brackets 2 and 3) during the measure. This idea is also used in measure 3, but the pattern moves down the fingerboard. The key to successfully employing this kind of chromaticism is resolution: as in measures 2 and 3, you start "inside" (on notes in the key or the scale), move "outside" (to notes not part of the harmony), and finally resolve back to a note in the chord or key.

72 Fig. 123

CHAPTER 11

EXOTIC SCALES

The exotic scales here offer an interesting alternative to the major, minor, blues, and pentatonic scales that most rock and pop guitarists use. At first, they might sound a little strange, but after you experiment with the fingerings and feel confident with them, try to fit them into your soloing. To understand how to use these scales, it's helpful to know what scales they are related to. The Hungarian minor (Fig. 124A) is closely related to the harmonic minor; the Hindu (Fig. 125A) is similar to the Mixolydian mode; and the Japanese pentatonic (Fig. 126A) is similar to the Phrygian mode. So, say you have a progression that you normally solo over with A harmonic minor; you could use the A Hungarian minor as well. Even if these related scales or modes are not all that familiar, the figures below will help you get an idea of what kinds of progressions the exotic scales will work with.

Each figure includes two fingerings of the scale followed by a riff. Once you have the scales down, you can use them to improvise over the riffs.

 Figs. 124A & 124B

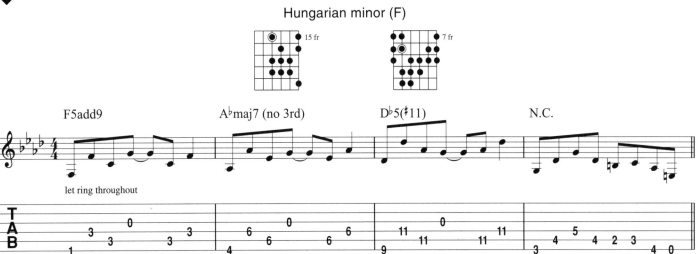

 Figs. 125A & 125B

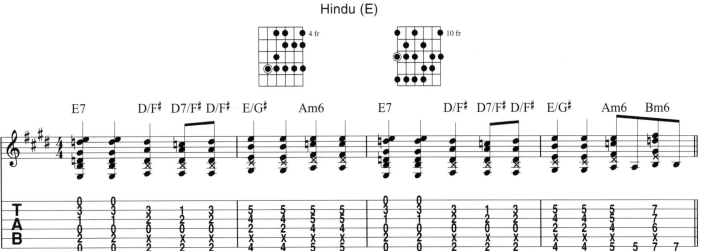

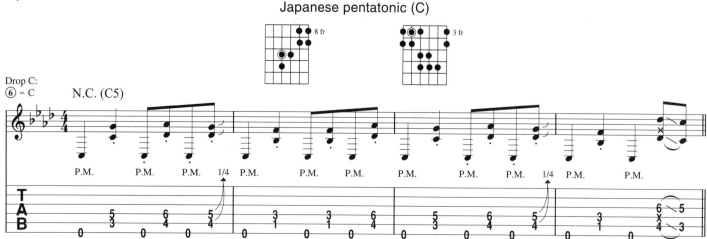

Japanese pentatonic (C)

The riff in Fig. 126B features a dropped C tuning. To achieve this, simply detune string 6 down to a C; you can determine that the pitch is correct by making sure the detuned string matches the C note on the third fret of the fifth string.

HYBRID SCALES

You can create a unique harmonic source for your solos by combining the notes in two different scales. When you do this, the result often doesn't have an official name—hence the term "hybrid."

Although you could combine almost any two scales into a hybrid, the first one we will focus on involves notes from the A minor pentatonic (A–C–D–E–G) and A major pentatonic (A–B–C♯–E–F♯). Fig. 127 shows you a fingering for each of these scales. The third fingering is the scale that results when you combine them—the scale we will call the A minor/major pentatonic hybrid (A–B–C–C♯–D–E–F♯–G). The notes in boxes in this fingering represent the notes of an A7 chord (A–C♯–E–G); soloists tend to emphasize these when they use this kind of scale. The rationale behind this hybrid is simple: when players solo over a dominant seventh chord, they generally create phrases with the minor pentatonic or the major pentatonic. So it makes sense to create a hybrid that is based on these two scales.

Fig. 127

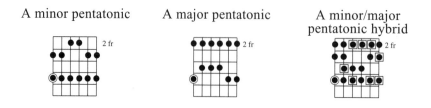

A minor pentatonic   A major pentatonic   A minor/major pentatonic hybrid

The lick in Fig. 128 uses the hybrid scale fingering.

Fig. 128

The hybrid scale in Fig. 129 combines the A major pentatonic scale and the A blues scale (A–C–D–E♭–E–G), also commonly used over an A7 chord. When combined, they form the A blues/major pentatonic hybrid scale (A–B–C–C♯–D–E♭–E–F♯–G).

Fig. 129

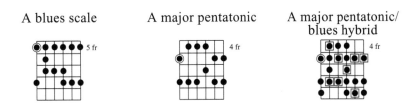

Because this new scale has nine notes, it can seem a bit unwieldy. But remember, when you solo with this (or any scale for that matter), there is no need to use all the notes. Again, you can emphasize the notes in an A7 chord (the notes in boxes). Examine the licks in Figs. 128 and 130 to see how they favor these notes—and notice that neither lick uses all the notes in the scale.

 Fig. 130

CHAPTER 13

CREATING RHYTHMIC DIVERSITY

Here we look at two important and related aspects of sophisticated improvising: the ability to move effortlessly between different rhythms, and the ability to be free from basing all your solo rhythms on the underlying rhythmic unit of the song—be it an eighth note, a sixteenth note, or a shuffle groove (swung eighth notes). In other words, even if the song is a shuffle, you might want to switch back and forth between swung and straight eighth notes.

The exercises in Figs. 131–133 can help you develop these abilities. At first, you might experience some trouble moving from eighth-note triplets (three notes per beat) to sixteenth notes (four notes per beat). But if you count the beats out and practice the figures slowly, it's not too tough. Players can sometimes have difficulty with the quintuplet (five notes played in the space of a quarter note) in Fig. 133. But an easy way to determine the rhythm of this grouping is to insert a five syllable word, such as "hip-po-pot-a-mus," into a beat. You could create a number of exercises similar to these figures—you could change every beat from eighth-note triplets to quintuplets or use any other combination you can think of.

 Fig. 131

 Fig. 132

 Fig. 133

Another and perhaps stranger way to come up with new rhythms might seem a little like math homework: take a measure comprised entirely of eighth-note triplets and randomly remove some of the notes. Written out, a measure would first look like this: 123, 223, 323, 423. But after I take out some beats so that every quarter-note has a different rhythmic unit, one possible result is: 1-3, -23, 32-, 423. I do the same for a second measure, and end up with -23, 223, -2-, -23. I then combine this rhythm and the hybrid scale from Fig. 74D [Chapter 7] to come up with Fig. 134. Try this technique with other rhythms, such as quarter-note triplets or sixteenth-notes; you will definitely come up with some cool rhythms that you wouldn't normally play. After working with these ideas, begin to incorporate them into your solos. Eventually, you will find that they have become a natural part of your playing.

 Fig. 134

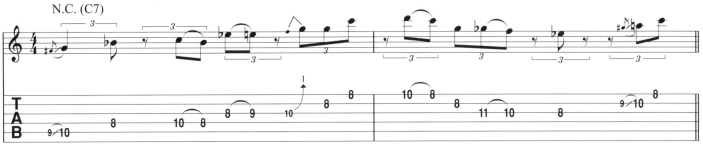

RHYTHMIC GROUPINGS

When working with three-note groups, it's easy to play them as triplets. And it's equally easy to play four-note patterns as sixteenth notes. Yet you can create interesting rhythmic feels by putting an odd-numbered note pattern into an even-numbered rhythm, or vice versa.

We begin in Fig. 135 with a two-note sequence similar to Fig. 112 [Chapter 12]. In measures 1 and 2, you play the pattern in a straightforward way: the two-note sequence is played as two eighth notes. But in measures 3 and 4, you play the sequence as eighth-note triplets. This slight change gives the same sequence a totally different feel.

 Fig. 135

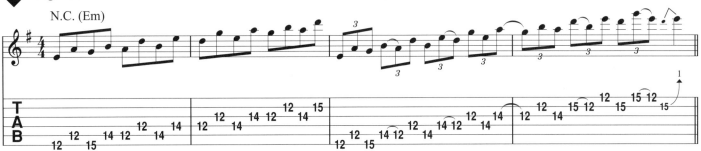

The first measure of Fig. 136 contains triad arpeggios played as triplets—this is fairly typical. But in measure 2, the same arpeggios are played as sixteenth notes. In measure 1 each three-note group starts on the beat, yet when played as sixteenth notes, however, each group (indicated by brackets) begins on a different beat; the first sixteenth of the beat, the fourth sixteenth, the third, and the second, respectively. You can draw attention to the new grouping by accenting the first note of each group. And because each pattern begins on a different subdivision of the beat, the accent will continuously shift. I have provided some picking suggestions, but feel free to experiment with other methods if this is not comfortable for you.

 Fig. 136

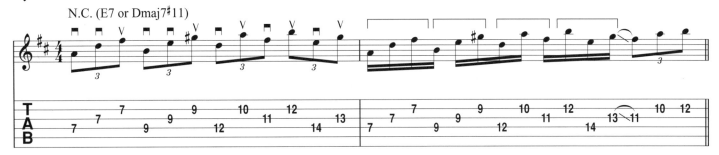

You can apply the same idea to four-note groups as well. In Fig. 137, we play the pattern first as sixteenth notes and then as triplets.

 Fig. 137

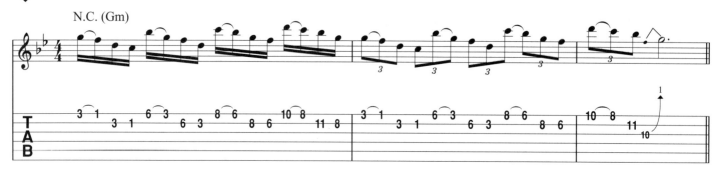

Experiment with other combinations, such as five-note patterns played as triplets and five- and seven-note patterns played as sixteenth notes. You can also create an interesting effect by inserting a rest in place of one note within any of these patterns. As any good player will tell you, a rest can be just as important in a phrase as any note: What you don't play is often as important as what you do play.

CHAPTER 16

CREATING MELODIC LINES THROUGH CHORD CHANGES

You can bring an added level of sophistication to your solos by learning how to create melodic lines that closely follow the chord changes. One way to start building such lines is by determining the half-step connections between the chords in a progression. In Fig. 138, when the Gm7 (G–B♭–D–F) moves to the E♭9 (E♭–G–B♭–D♭–F), we have two choices: D up to E♭, or D down to D♭. When the E♭9 moves to the C9 (C–E–G–B♭–D) we have numerous choices: D♭ to C, D♭ to D, F to E, E♭ to E. Although we could go from E to F when the chords move from C9 to Gm7, for the sake of variety we connect the C in the C9 to the B♭ in the Gm7 with a chromatic passing tone (B). And finally, we return to the half-step connection formula as we move from G to F♯ to connect the Gm7 to the D7 (D–F♯–A–C). But half-step connections are not the only way you can tie this progression (or others) together. Almost all these chords have two "common tones": G and B♭. You could create a phrase that repeats or holds one or both of these notes while the chords change. Because you have so many options, as you solo over this progression try changing the way you connect the chords.

85 **Fig. 138**

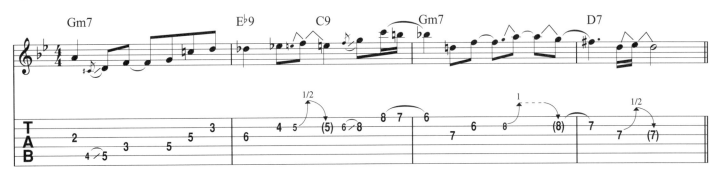

In Fig. 139, we move between E7 (E–G♯–B–D) and A7 (A–C♯–E–G). These chords have two half-step connections: G♯ to G and D to C♯. But rather than playing the second note of the connection on the beat (as we did in Fig. 138), here we either rhythmically anticipate or delay the resolution by playing before or after the chord change actually occurs (the arrows indicate the anticipated or delayed chord notes).

86 **Fig. 139**

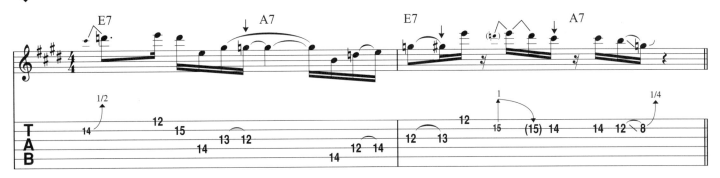

Fig. 140 puts all of the above ideas together. It employs half-step connections, common tones, and rhythmic anticipation, and it uses whole-step connections as well. Measure 1 connects to measure 2 via a whole step: as the chords move from A (A–C♯–E) to C (C–E–G), the solo line moves from A to G. The next two connections are a half step (G to F♯) and a whole step (D to C). The chord progression repeats in the next four bars, but for the sake of variety, here the A is emphasized—a common tone within D (D–F♯–A) and F (F–A–C).

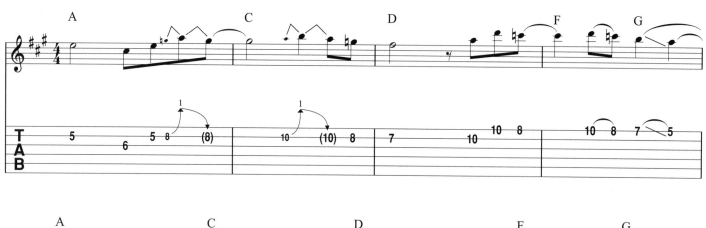

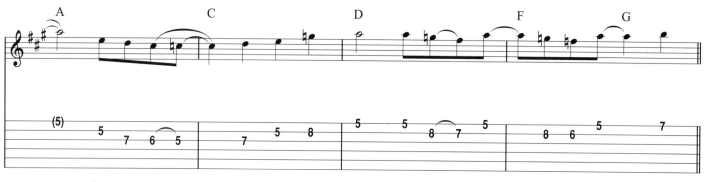

CHAPTER 17

NATURAL HARMONICS

Natural harmonics are great for producing chime-like sounds. They occur most prominently at the frets 5, 7, and 12. To execute a natural harmonic, place any finger of your fretting hand directly over the fret wire at the fifth, seventh, or twelfth fret on any string, making sure that your finger touches the string (and not the fingerboard) as lightly as possible. Pick that string and then quickly lift your finger.

To know what kind of progressions these harmonics could be used with, you need to know what notes they produce. When you play a harmonic at the fifth or twelfth fret, the note produced is the same note (in a higher octave) as the open string you are playing. So, for example, playing the twelfth fret harmonic on each string from low to high results in the notes E–A–D–G–B–E. Harmonics at the twelfth fret produce a note that is the octave higher than the open string, while harmonics at the fifth fret produce a note that is two octaves higher than the open string. When you play natural harmonics at the seventh fret, the note produced is an octave and a 5th above the open string. So, playing the seventh fret harmonic on each string from low to high results in the notes B–E–A–D–F#–B. Note that whereas twelfth fret harmonics produce the exact same tone as the twelfth fret played normally, seventh fret harmonics produce a tone one octave higher than the seventh fret played normally.

While you can play harmonics as individual notes, you can also play them as chords. Fig. 141 shows six chords and two m7 arpeggios that can be played solely with harmonics.

Fig. 141

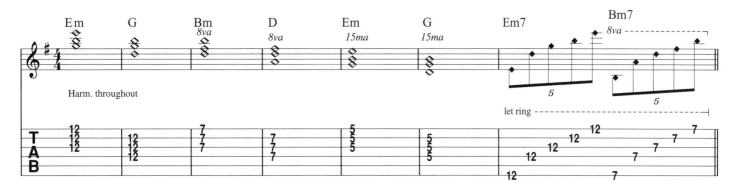

Fig. 142 employs fretted notes in conjunction with harmonics. When you play this figure, make sure that all the notes ring throughout the measure. In measure 1, for instance, you need to hold the C (tenth fret, fourth string) down with your finger while you play the following harmonics.

 Fig. 142

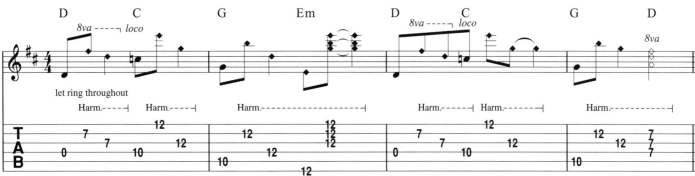

Notice how in Fig. 143 the combination of regular notes and harmonics results in chords like Cadd9(#11)—a chord that can not be played with just harmonics.

89 **Fig. 143**

Although we have focused on the fifth, seventh, and twelfth frets, harmonics can be played at many other frets. At most of these locations, however, the harmonic tends to be more difficult to produce—you might have to pick the string harder than normal in order to make the harmonic ring strongly. Using the bridge-position pickup on your guitar will greatly enhance the ability to produce harmonics clearly. Try playing a harmonic at the fourth fret on the low E string. Once you can get this note to sound, play harmonics on this string at the fourth, fifth, and seventh frets. The notes you produce—G#, E, and B, respectively—form an E chord. This same procedure on the A string gives you the notes C#, A, and E, the notes in an A chord (A–C#–E). On the D string, the notes produced are F#, D, A, the notes in a D chord (D–F#–A). When you are creating a riff with the chords E, A, and D, try to work in these harmonics.

HARP HARMONICS

Because of the particular pitches they produce, natural harmonics tend to fit only a few keys and chords—most notably G, D, Em, and Bm. But *harp* harmonics allow you to play harmonics, scales, complex chords, and bends in any key.

The following figures are some of the most difficult in the book because they require you to use your picking hand in a way that might initially feel awkward. But, as with any difficult exercise, patience is the key. Don't expect to master these harmonics without a fair amount of practice.

There are two possible ways to play harp harmonics:

1) Hold the pick between the thumb and middle finger. This leaves the index finger on this hand free to touch the string above the appropriate fret.

2) Play them without a pick. Your index finger on the picking hand touches the string above the appropriate fret, and either your thumb or one of your other fingers on the same hand plucks the string.

The technique will become clear in the figures below. You should experiment with methods 1 and 2 on these figures and then decide which feels best to you.

Fig. 144 uses two familiar chord shapes played with harp harmonics. The chord diagram above each measure shows the chord your fretting hand will play. Your picking hand simply traces the shape of the chord with your index finger, which lightly touches the string (above the fret wire) twelve frets higher than the note you are fretting. So, for the first note of this figure, your fretting hand plays an F (third fret, fourth string). The index finger on your picking hand lightly touches the same string (but not the fingerboard) directly above the fret twelve frets higher (fret 15). You then strike the string using either method one or two. Repeat this technique for all the notes in this figure. As you are getting comfortable with harp harmonics, work on Fig. 144 slowly. Play it one measure at a time and repeat each measure until all the notes ring clearly.

Fig. 144

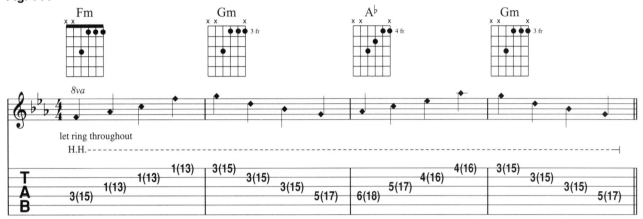

Fig. 145 uses a few more chords to create a figure that is a bit more difficult.

90 **Fig. 145**

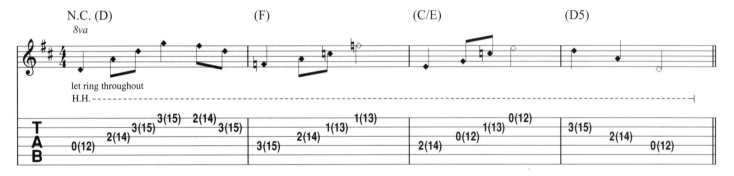

Harp harmonics can also be used on solo lines. For example, the lick in Fig. 146 uses notes from a G minor pentatonic scale (G–B♭–C–D–F) in conjunction with some bends. After you get these figures down, try this harp technique on any other scales, chords, or licks that you know.

91 **Fig. 146**

CHAPTER 18

JAZZ HARMONY AND COMPING

Although learning how to play jazz is a life-long pursuit, there are a number of ways to get a jazz sound without too much effort. Here we focus on a typical accompaniment part that a jazz guitarist might play.

The progression that forms the backbone of many jazz compositions is the ii–V. The ii–V is a series of chords built on the 2nd and 5th notes of a major or minor scale. So, in the key of C major (C–**D**–E–F–**G**–A–B) for example, the chords are built on D and G. The ii chord will be a minor 7th and the V chord will be a dominant 7th. In this key, the result is Dm7 (D–F–A–C) and G7 (G–B–D–F). In the case of C minor, the chords are built on the 2nd and 5th notes in a C harmonic minor scale (C–**D**–E♭–F–**G**–A♭–B). In C minor, then, the ii–V is Dm7♭5–G7. (Notice how the ii is different in the major and minor key, while the V is the same). When jazz guitarists play ii–V progressions, they often embellish the basic chords with additional notes or "extensions." So Dm7 to G7 might be played as Dm9 to G9, for instance.

Fig. 147 is an eight-bar progression typical of those in jazz "standards," songs commonly found in the jazz repertoire. Even though this figure uses many different chords, it is still based on the ii-V progression. In order to generate all these chords, though, the song goes through a number a different keys. The symbols underneath the staff provide a measure by measure analysis of the key that each chord comes from. The letter before the colon indicates the key, and the Roman numerals identify the chord's relationship to that key. (Notice that in measure 7, the Am7 chord can be played as an A7.) Knowing the key that each chord comes from is important; it helps you decide what notes to play over each chord.

Fig. 147

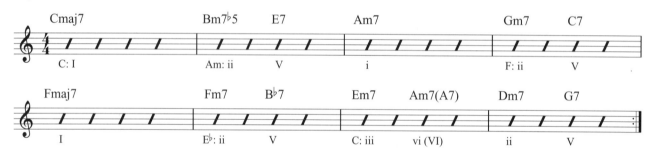

Typically, jazz "comping" (short for accompanying) leaves more space and is less rhythmically repetitive than conventional rock/pop guitar parts. Fig. 148 shows you one way a jazz guitarist might play the progression from Fig. 147.

 Fig. 148

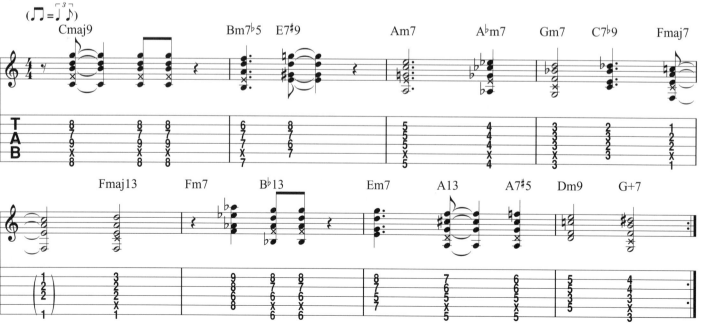

Fig. 149 gives you another set of typical jazz voicings that you could use over this progression—experiment with applying different rhythms to these chords. Notice how many of the chords in these two figures use the substitution ideas from Chapter 3 [Expanding Your Harmonic Vocabulary]. Play these figures two ways: with a pick, and with your fingers.

93 **Fig. 149**

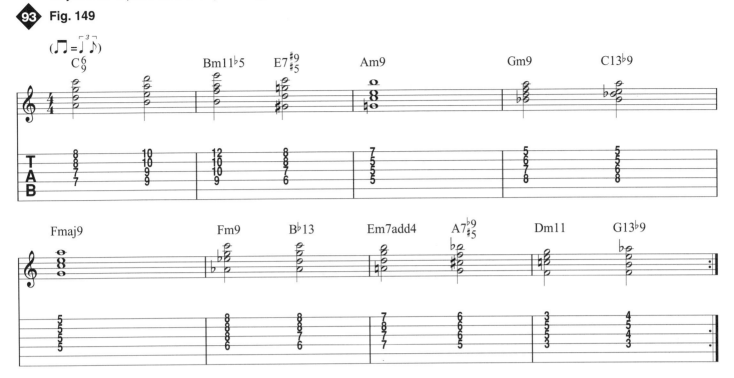

JAZZ SOLOING

In the previous section, we looked at the basics of jazz chord progressions and some typical jazz comping parts. Here we learn a little about jazz soloing. We will play two eight-bar solos based on the set of changes we explored in Figs. 147–149. If some of the terms and the theory escape you, don't worry. You can get a lot out of these figures just by playing them.

Fig. 150 provides a breakdown of the progression and shows you a major or minor scale that works over each chord.

Fig. 150

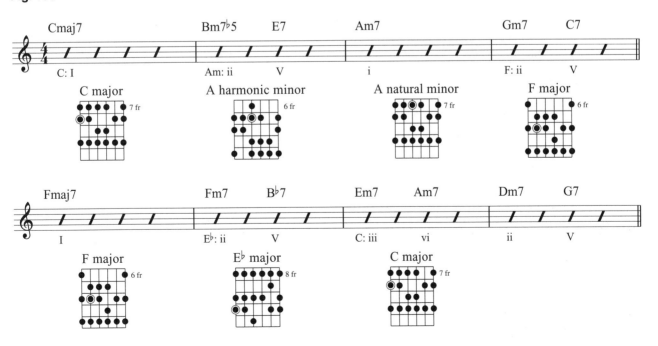

Using the scales and fingerings from Fig. 150, the solo in Fig. 151 moves through the chord changes diatonically: it never leaves the key that each chord comes from. Although this solo uses slides and slurs, some jazz players will pick every note. So try this figure (and Fig. 152) without the slides and slurs as well.

94 **Fig. 151**

While jazz players do play diatonically at times, they also tend to use a lot of chromatic notes to create tension and harmonic interest. Fig. 152 moves away from the key centers and scales used in Fig. 151 by employing notes called "alterations." These altered notes occur most commonly over V chords; typical alterations include the ♭9, ♯9, ♭5, and ♯5. This figure also utilizes arpeggios along with approach notes and chromatic passing notes (refer to Chapter 13 [Improvising With Chromatic Notes]).

95 **Fig. 152**

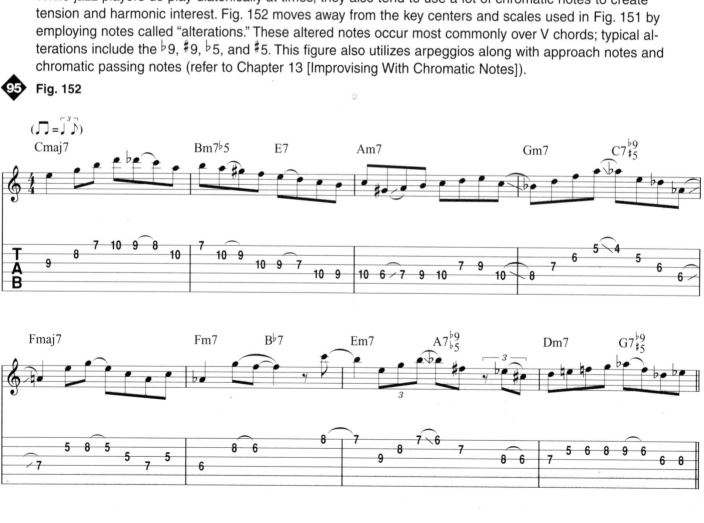

CHAPTER 19

ETUDE

Although the three figures here are ultimately intended to be combined together into one piece, I have divided the etude based on the type of riffs that each section uses. You can think of these figures as a kind of warehouse of ideas; the arpeggios and riffs you learn from working on these figures can be applied elsewhere.

As much as possible, Fig. 153 should be played with alternate picking (down-up-down-up). But because this method is not always the most effective one, I have provided suggestions at locations where you might have some doubt as to the best way to pick it. These are only suggestions—experiment until you find the way that seems best to you.

 Fig. 153 (Figs. 153–156 all appear on audio track 96)

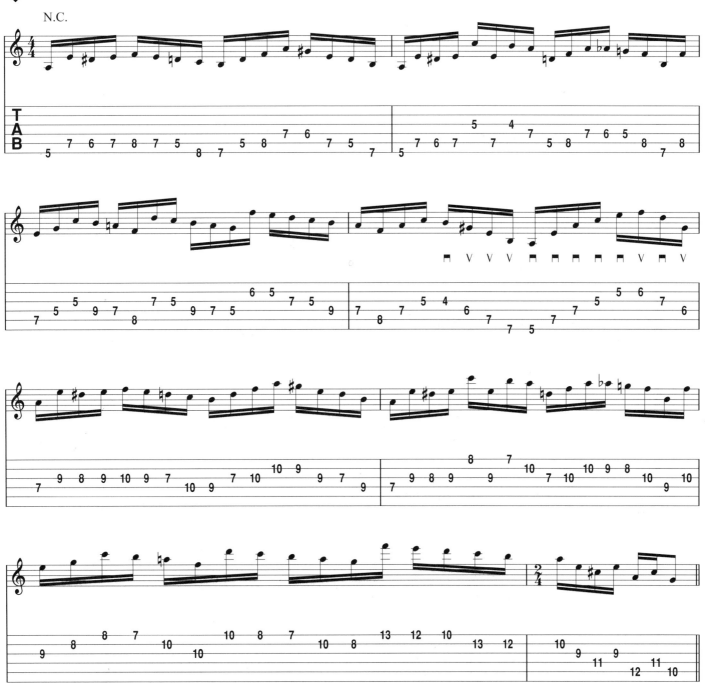

In Fig. 154, I have circled the root notes of each arpeggio (in the tablature notation) so that you'll be able to transpose the arpeggio and determine its root (refer to the Fingerboard Note Names chart at the beginning of this book). I have provided some picking suggestions here, as well.

Fig. 154

In Fig. 155, you should return to strict alternate picking.

Fig. 155

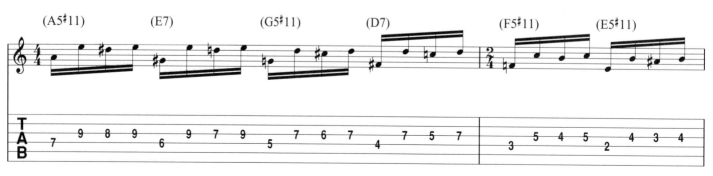

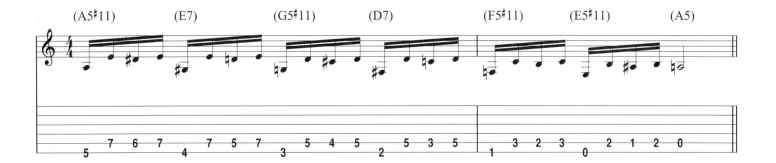

BIG ARPEGGIOS

In Chapter 9, we played major and minor arpeggios in three- and four-note groups. Here (Fig. 156) we look at four-, five-, six-, seven-, and eight-note arpeggios based on complex chord qualities, such as the m9 in measure 1 and the m11 in measure 3.

97 Fig. 156

When first working on this figure, don't allow any of the notes to ring—you might even palm mute all of them. After you feel comfortable with the fingerings, try to let as many notes as possible ring together. For the first three notes in measure 1, for example, hold down your first, second, and then fourth fingers. When you have to move your first finger to play the note on the second string, keep holding the second and fourth fingers down. When you play the note on the first string with your third finger, your second, third, and fourth fingers should be holding notes. Even though holding notes while moving other fingers can be difficult, try to keep as many fingers down as you can, even if it's only one. Don't worry if you can't get them all—that's often nearly impossible to do.

SOLO GUITAR: "BLACK IS THE COLOR OF MY TRUE LOVE'S HAIR"

Here we work on the traditional folk song, "Black is the Color of My True Love's Hair," arranged for solo guitar (Fig. 157). This arrangement, though, is not a typical folk adaptation. Taking some liberties with the song, we use conventions of rock and pop guitar, such as power chords and blues scales. Although many solo guitar pieces require that you have a high level of skill with fingerpicking, this arrangement is designed to be played with a pick.

 Fig. 157

GUITAR NOTATION LEGEND

Guitar Music can be notated three different ways: on a *musical staff*, in *tablature*, and in *rhythm slashes*.

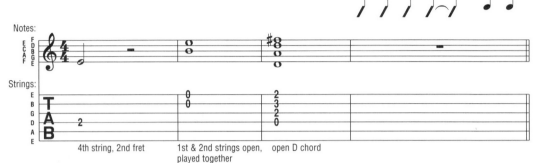

RHYTHM SLASHES are written above the staff. Strum chords in the rhythm indicated. Use the chord diagrams found at the top of the first page of the transcription for the appropriate chord voicings. Round noteheads indicate single notes.

THE MUSICAL STAFF shows pitches and rhythms and is divided by bar lines into measures. Pitches are named after the first seven letters of the alphabet.

TABLATURE graphically represents the guitar fingerboard. Each horizontal line represents a string, and each number represents a fret.

4th string, 2nd fret   1st & 2nd strings open, played together   open D chord

HALF-STEP BEND: Strike the note and bend up 1/2 step.

WHOLE-STEP BEND: Strike the note and bend up one step.

GRACE NOTE BEND: Strike the note and bend up as indicated. The first note does not take up any time.

SLIGHT (MICROTONE) BEND: Strike the note and bend up 1/4 step.

BEND AND RELEASE: Strike the note and bend up as indicated, then release back to the original note. Only the first note is struck.

PRE-BEND: Bend the note as indicated, then strike it.

VIBRATO: The string is vibrated by rapidly bending and releasing the note with the fretting hand.

WIDE VIBRATO: The pitch is varied to a greater degree by vibrating with the fretting hand.

HAMMER-ON: Strike the first (lower) note with one finger, then sound the higher note (on the same string) with another finger by fretting it without picking.

PULL-OFF: Place both fingers on the notes to be sounded. Strike the first note and without picking, pull the finger off to sound the second (lower) note.

LEGATO SLIDE: Strike the first note and then slide the same fret-hand finger up or down to the second note. The second note is not struck.

SHIFT SLIDE: Same as legato slide, except the second note is struck.

TRILL: Very rapidly alternate between the notes indicated by continuously hammering on and pulling off.

TAPPING: Hammer ("tap") the fret indicated with the pick-hand index or middle finger and pull off to the note fretted by the fret hand.

NATURAL HARMONIC: Strike the note while the fret-hand lightly touches the string directly over the fret indicated.

PINCH HARMONIC: The note is fretted normally and a harmonic is produced by adding the edge of the thumb or the tip of the index finger of the pick hand to the normal pick attack.

PICK SCRAPE: The edge of the pick is rubbed down (or up) the string, producing a scratchy sound.

MUFFLED STRINGS: A percussive sound is produced by laying the fret hand across the string(s) without depressing, and striking them with the pick hand.

PALM MUTING: The note is partially muted by the pick hand lightly touching the string(s) just before the bridge.

RAKE: Drag the pick across the strings indicated with a single motion.

TREMOLO PICKING: The note is picked as rapidly and continuously as possible.

VIBRATO BAR DIVE AND RETURN: The pitch of the note or chord is dropped a specified number of steps (in rhythm) then returned to the original pitch.

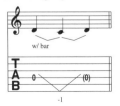

VIBRATO BAR SCOOP: Depress the bar just before striking the note, then quickly release the bar.

VIBRATO BAR DIP: Strike the note and then immediately drop a specified number of steps, then release back to the original pitch.